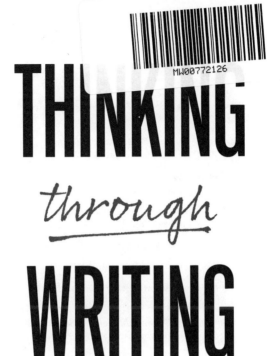

THINKING

through

WRITING

Skills for Scholars

THINKING

through

WRITING

A Guide to Becoming a
Better Writer & Thinker

John Kaag &
Jonathan van Belle

Princeton University Press
Princeton and Oxford

Published by Princeton University Press
41 William Street, Princeton, New Jersey 08540
99 Banbury Road, Oxford OX2 6JX

press.princeton.edu

Library of Congress Cataloging-in-Publication Data

Names: Kaag, John, 1979– author. | van Belle, Jonathan, author.
Title: Thinking through writing : a guide to becoming a better writer and
    thinker / John Kaag, Jonathan van Belle.
Description: Princeton : Princeton University Press, [2024] |
    Includes index.
Identifiers: LCCN 2023047063 (print) | LCCN 2023047064 (ebook) |
    ISBN 9780691249599 (hardback) | ISBN 9780691249582 (paperback) |
    ISBN 9780691249605 (ebook)
Subjects: LCSH: English language—Rhetoric—Handbooks, manuals, etc |
    English language—Composition and exercises. | Authorship—
    Technique. | Critical thinking. | BISAC: LANGUAGE ARTS &
    DISCIPLINES / Writing / Composition | EDUCATION / Reference
Classification: LCC PE1408 .K23 2024 (print) | LCC PE1408 (ebook) |
    DDC 808/.042—dc23/eng/20240102
LC record available at https://lccn.loc.gov/2023047063
LC ebook record available at https://lccn.loc.gov/2023047064

British Library Cataloging-in-Publication Data is available

Editorial: Matt Rohal and Alena Chekanov
Production Editorial: Natalie Baan
Text Design: Wanda España
Production: Erin Suydam
Copyeditor: Hank Southgate

This book has been composed in Pulpo

Printed in the United States of America

10 9 8 7 6 5 4 3 2 1

For my students, 3,111 and happily counting.

John Kaag

To Zuriel.

Jonathan van Belle

No tears in the writer, no tears in the reader.

—Robert Frost, "The Figure a Poem Makes,"
preface to *Collected Poems of Robert Frost*

About the Authors

John Kaag is the Donahue Professor of Ethics and the Arts at the University of Massachusetts Lowell and external professor at the Santa Fe Institute. Between 2010 and 2016, he was visiting assistant professor of writing at Harvard University. He is the author of *Sick Souls, Healthy Minds: How William James Can Save Your Life* (Princeton).

Jonathan van Belle is a writer and editor whose work has appeared in *Aeon, Fast Company, Times Higher Education,* and other publications. Kaag and van Belle are the coauthors of *Henry at Work: Thoreau on Making a Living* (Princeton).

Contents

4 THINKING THROUGH OTHERS   121

5 THINKING THROUGH THE SELF   141

6 THINKING THROUGH EVIDENCE   167

THINKING

through

WRITING

Introduction

THINKING THROUGH WRITING

Let us "think through writing" together. To do this, we will think about the ways we can write, why we might want to communicate with writing, what we hope to convey, and how we sometimes fail. This also means that we think about how we read, when to ask questions, what questions to ask, what to outline, where to make an argument, and which words need to be placed in what order. Thinking through writing is an invitation to consider the intimate relationship between "right" thinking and the creative, critical, semimiraculous act of writing. Essentially, that is what *Thinking through Writing* is all about.

When it comes to learning how to negotiate the world and navigate your future classes in thoughtful ways, it is not always helpful, much less ideal, to be taught how to write in one book and how to think critically in another. Yet that is how most books are organized—into two categories, the writing guides and the critical thinking handbooks. We do things differently in this book: in *Thinking through Writing*, we offer a concise and practical manual for developing reading, writing, and thinking skills in tandem. With short, manageable, and practical chapters, our book is intended to get you to think critically about yourself and the world at large, to read carefully and get the necessary literary support, to write clearly and persuasively, to stay on point, and to finish your work as cleanly and compellingly as possible.

Drawing on a decade of teaching Harvard's Freshman Expository Writing Course, as well as developing philosophy courses on writing and critical thinking for a variety of online and in-person classes, this book provides a personal and impassioned guide to writing and critical thinking for those who need to form arguments at the university and beyond. We will also draw on a variety of perspectives and tips from interviews with some of the most interesting and brilliant writers working today, in addition to exercises and templates in critical thinking and writing to get you to realize your full potential in practice. If education is training for the "real world," then *Thinking through Writing* is training for one's life in the real world of thinking critically and writing well.

Thinking through Writing is the Swiss Army knife of college-level writing and critical thinking. If you've ever been at a loss for words, you should read this book. If you want to make an argument, but don't know where to start or how to end, you should read this book. If you struggle to support your ideas, to provide evidence that convinces and compels, you should read this book.

At one point or another, we all need to express in written words our own thinking, and this is a manual or handbook for these pivotal moments. *Thinking through Writing* is spring training for your life in the world of words, images, and arguments. Practice does not make perfect, but it does enable progress: reading, writing, and thinking are skills that can be taught. And those who fail to take the time to learn will miss the rare and therefore precious opportunity to make their mark.

Students are often quoted as saying that the whole point of college is to get through it as quickly as possible in order to enter "the real world." The real testing ground for our minds, some assume, will be found in adulthood. There may be some truth to this, but here's the rub: by the time you reach the "real testing ground" of mature life, it is, in one sense, a heavier lift to think critically. The more fluid flow of intelligence in one's youth crystallizes with age, which makes learning new and challenging ideas harder (though not impossible—far from it!). We think the best time to acquire skills is always as soon as possible. One of the greatest, if not the greatest, mathematician-philosophers of the last one hundred years, Alfred North Whitehead, warned against such delays and deferrals:

> The mind is never passive; it is a perpetual activity, delicate, receptive, responsive to stimulus. You cannot postpone its life until you have sharpened it. Whatever interest attaches to your subject-matter must be evoked here and now; whatever powers you are strengthening in the pupil, must be exercised here and now; whatever possibilities of mental life your teaching should impart, must be exhibited here and now. That is the golden rule of education, and a very difficult rule to follow.[1]

We offer a guide on writing and critical thinking that is meant to appeal to your "delicate, receptive, responsive" mind. We aim to evoke your interest, through enjoyable examples, strengthen your powers, through creative exercises, and nourish your mental life "here and now." You have the power to communicate something vitally important to your reader or listener, to your audience both immediate and imagined, but you may need help to hone that power.

We are all rhetoricians—to greater or lesser extent—as soon as we learn to gesture or speak. Our minds and our words are fellow travelers. Plato, in the voice of Socrates questioning Phaedrus, an Athenian aristocrat, puts to us

---

1. Alfred North Whitehead, *The Aims of Education and Other Essays*, rev. ed. (London: Williams & Norgate, 1950), 9.

these questions about rhetoric: "Is not the art of rhetoric a method of influencing men's minds by means of words, whether the words are spoken in a court of law or before some other public body or in private conversation? And is not the same art involved whatever the importance of the subject under discussion, so that it is no more creditable to use it correctly on a serious matter than on a trifle?"[2] In other words, rhetoric is everywhere, and its power affects us in everything we do. Plato's most famous student, Aristotle, suggested that we can persuade others in three distinct ways: we can appeal to an audience's character (*ethos*), to their emotions (*pathos*), and to their reason (*logos*). Let's think through that viewpoint.

If you've ever tried to get a child to eat their vegetables, you can argue on the basis of character ("Be a good boy, listen to your Mama, and down those carrots"), or you can appeal to their emotions and scare them into it ("If you don't eat your carrots, your Dear Old Dad will send a horrible monster to get you in the night"), or you can appeal to their sense of reasoning and craft a practical argument ("Eating your carrots will help your stomach feel good tomorrow"). In each case, you take a slightly different rhetorical stance, but with the common objective of changing a listener's mind—and getting those carrots eaten before you go insane. You don't want to fight with the kid—resorting to physical violence or threat won't do, no matter how tempting it is—instead you want to give an argument that changes the little bugger's mood, and then their mind, and then their actions. Ideally, at the end of the argument, an audience will actually want to change their mind, or not even notice that they have already. In a fight,

---

2. Plato, *Phaedrus*, trans. Walter Hamilton (New York: Penguin Books, 1995), 52–53.

you try to win, to destroy, to humiliate. In an argument, you try to entice a listener to agree with you. That is what becoming an effective rhetorician and writer means.

Argument by Character (ethos): This is the attempt to persuade a listener by presenting yourself as the sort of speaker they could and should trust. People care about people (it is sort of in our interpersonal DNA). When you make an argument by character, you are presenting yourself as the "informed and responsible adult" to your audience, the sort of person they can believe in.

Argument by Emotion (pathos): You know what else is in our interpersonal DNA? The capacity to *feel something* on the basis of the words we hear or read. Manipulating the emotions of a listener sounds more devious than it has to be. Start by thinking about the feelings of your audience and figure out how to recognize those fears and desires to make your point. Logic can only get you so far, but as we know from as far back as the Romantics of the early nineteenth century, something in the "gut," so to speak, is often what moves us to action.

Argument by Logic (logos): Think of arguments as co-workers. Some you really respect (arguments by character), and some you fear or desperately want to date (arguments by emotion). But then there are the nerdy ones who are always there with the right answer and all the right evidence. Meet the argument by logic: it persuades by sound reasoning, but, more helpfully, figures out what reasons will matter to a particular audience and lays them out cogently.

Plato believed that being fully human involved an active commitment to three interlocking ideals: the True, the Good, and the Beautiful. We are, in life, supposed to speak and write on behalf of these ideals. No one thinker can ever understand these ideas in their entirety, which is why we spend so much of our lives talking things out, trying, for example, to get as real as we can. Rhetoric, at its base, assumes that certain aspects of our world deserve to be reconceived, revised, and reworked. And here is the amazing thing about words: when we put them in the right order—in an argument—they can change moods, minds, and actions. This, in turn, can change the world.

So rhetoric, critical thinking, and composition are important, even vitally so. For consider the alternative: to live a thoughtless, easy life, in which you are manipulated by someone else's words, taken in by their bullshit, used for their purposes, and defined by their vision of reality. No, thank you. So, if thinking through our words seems tough, just remember what the stakes are. Now let's get to work.

BECOMING A WRITER AND THINKER

When John was a teenager, his single mother, Becky, called him into the kitchen with a very simple invitation: "Why don't you do your *writing* homework in the kitchen? Just *think* about it a little more, John." He was in the middle of a horrible essay for his high-school English class. Becky, who was doing the dishes at the sink, was a substitute English teacher. From that point forth, night after night, John took to the small round table in central Pennsylvania to join his first writing-thinking coach to train him in this crucial art. He needed help: he was a stuttering, shy student who hated to read and write. He just couldn't get his ideas in the right order. He also was more than a little bit arrogant and even inflammatory, which meant that even if he did get his ideas in the right order, no one was going to listen to him. Before they started, his mother-teacher gave John some advice that seems like the very best way to start a crash course in writing and critical thinking: "John," she said, "becoming a better writer involves becoming a better person. Don't take this the wrong way, but before you pick up that pen, you need to become more thoughtful." What did his English teacher want to see in the essay? What was she like as a person? What did she think was most important about the book they had been reading in class? This was a not-so-subtle way of encouraging her son to acknowledge his audience—their values, interests, and concerns—and then to approach his audience accordingly, gently and persuasively. In short, she urged him to become the sort of rhetor-writer people wanted to listen to and like.

This took a while. Exactly how long is a matter of dispute. But after her first lesson, John's mother offered another: "When you have an idea, write it down." It seemed so simple, but it's really not. So many ideas—original, horrible, even brilliant but not fully formed—go extinct only because we never document their short lives. Some deserve to go the way of the dodo or woolly mammoth, but others don't, and those are the ones worth mourning. So, write them down. That was the advice of John's mother. And she gave him two very practical gifts that we would like you to afford yourself. The first was a pen—and not just any pen, a Pilot 233, a $1.50 rollerball (which was a fortune in his family)—and the second was a new notebook that he had permission to write anything he wanted in.

Times have changed, but the idea hasn't: become a writer by acting like one. If you have your own version of the Pilot 233, we promise you it will increase the chances that you put words to the page. Buy something that is just expensive enough that you will really miss it—and curse your bad luck when you misplace it—but not so expensive that you can't replace it. The experience of laying down ink should be a pleasure. If you have never owned such a pen, then it is high time. Keep it in a pocket and don't put it through the washing machine. If you don't wear pants with pockets, then clip it to your waistband.

What should you write in that notebook? We would not recommend writing "whatever," as John's mother did. That led to a half a life of wondering whether he was writing about the right things. Instead, we would suggest that you write down what is already in your head. Say you are stuck in traffic for fifteen minutes. What are you thinking about? (Be honest.) When you arrive at your destination, before you get out of the car, write it down in two sentences that start in the following way: "I am thinking _____. I am thinking _____, because _____." This is an easy method to begin thinking about logical structure and reasoning. It is also a good way to document over time trends in your thought-life that often go unnoticed. If you do this once a day for a month, you will observe patterns in your own thought ("Who knew I was thinking about waffles that much!") and omissions ("I should really think about my brother's feelings more"). From here, take a look at the boxed exercise that will be your first real chance to think through writing in a meaningful argument. Expressing a meaningful argument involves the delicate balancing act between taking your audience's concerns and interests seriously and being audacious enough to think that you can change their minds. Expressing an argument also involves knowing exactly what one is, to see it emerge on the page.

In ancient Rome, shopkeepers would put mosaics at the opening of their shops that read "caveat emptor," or "buyer beware," which warned shoppers to look carefully at the wares of the store and make sure that they were

Get to Work

USING A WRITER'S JOURNAL

What you have just created is a writer's journal. When the renowned nature writer Henry David Thoreau was a young man, his mentor Ralph Waldo Emerson approached him with a question: Do you keep a journal? Thoreau began, and by the end of his life his journal edged toward two million words. Let's start with a just few dozen words. We suggest that you try to write down your thoughts on an argument that recently bothered you, really pissed you off. Pick the one that you had with your sibling or partner, your colleague or your housemate. Write down both of your positions in that little journal of yours. Then list all the reasons you both (not just you) had for thinking that your position was the right one. Your opponent's reasons may seem stupid, but they probably aren't. They just aren't *your* reasons. So, write all of them down, if only in the name of fairness. The entry that you have made in your journal details, in a very rudimentary way, the structure of an argument that occupied your mind for some reason. The positions that you described are the conclusions that you and your opponent advanced. The reasons for believing you were right are the premises or supporting claims in your arguments. Now, three more steps:

1. Write the word "motivation" at the top of the page (or below your reasons if you don't have space). Next to it, in three sentences, write the reason you think the argument mattered to you and the person you were arguing with.
2. Next to each premise, write one piece of evidence that could be (or actually was) presented to support it.
3. Finally at the bottom, write out who won the argument and why.

getting what they wanted. So *"Caveat Emptor."* Get what you came for.

Thinking through Writing is familiar enough in organization that it will easily substitute for many books in both writing and critical thinking courses. The book emerged over the course of a decade teaching Harvard's Freshman Expository Writing Course, Expos 30. Every Expos preceptor at Harvard has to go through what is fondly known as "Expos Bootcamp," which is about the best prep course to teach college writing and critical thinking—to anybody who wants to form arguments in college and beyond. Kaag completed this training and went on to win Harvard's Bok Award for Teaching Excellence (awarded to 2 percent of the instructors each year). Blah, blah, blah—an argument from authority. "Now give me the real reason to read *Thinking through Writing*," you say. OK.

The rough and ready order of every Expos course at Harvard is as follows:

1. Close Reading
2. Analysis and Synthetic Reasoning
3. Asking Good Questions
4. Thesis Formation
5. Argument Structure (which includes all the baby logic and fallacy work you would ever want to do)
6. Assessing Evidence
7. Essay Structure (which includes everything from topic sentences to transitions)
8. Outlining
9. Entering a Critical Debate
10. Using Sources
11. Citations
12. Drafting and Revision

One thing should become clear: this course is about critical thinking (which includes critical reading) *and* writing. And one thing we want to make clear in *Thinking through Writing*: the skills and lessons in this book should be useful for those teaching and learning in the fields of writing *and* critical thinking. In part, this is the way that the authors of the guidebook in your hands became writers themselves.

Chapter 1

THINKING THROUGH THE BEGINNING

ENTERING A CRITICAL DEBATE

In thinking and writing, students and professionals almost always begin in the middle of things, thrown into an intellectual setting already on the move. More often than not, you have to find your way through a conversation that has been going on for a very long time, carried out by a diverse range of thinkers. And you will need to find the right words to respond to a host of critics and commentators who are interested in the same topics you are. History is brimming with authors who wrote a great deal about many things—which can be rather intimidating, even for the most seasoned authors. "How do I say anything new?" is a common feeling. Well, it is a good question, but a very answerable one. First, you need to understand what has already been said. In other words, to engage in an ongoing intellectual conversation, it is best to acquaint yourself with what is called a critical debate. It's important to remember that critical debates are encountered in virtually every piece of nonfiction writing that you will ever read—your own writing will fit within a critical debate, once you figure out which one you are interested in contributing to. The goal, then, of writing is to find your own place in the debate, use your voice, and make your own mark.

What Is a Critical Debate?

When we think, we are always thinking about something more or less specific, and often we think out loud to others, so our thoughts never arise in a vacuum. Writing and thinking are not acts of spontaneous generation, like conjuring something out of utter nothing; instead, writing and thinking take place in the context of an ongoing conversation or critical debate and address a particular issue. Critical debate (or critical analysis) involves two distinct moments: the process of carefully identifying and evaluating another person's ideas, positions, and arguments; and the process of expressing your own, with the full knowledge that they are about to be evaluated in a similar fashion. These debates can—and often do—span many years (decades, if not centuries) and address a variety of intellectual topics. Think of them as very long, respectful discussions about a controversial issue, which unfolds between some, generally speaking, smart and well-meaning people, the point of which is to develop greater insight about the nature of reality. At their best, these conversations form the foundation of human knowledge—cooperative, forward-looking, actionable, and revelatory.

The best writing contributes in some original way to an existing literature, even when it says something entirely original and new. The primary objective of writing is to make your mark—make a point, advance an argument, develop your own interpretation—but to do so requires that you make your mark in the midst of all the other marks that have already been made. One of the cool things about writing is making your thoughts visible—a type of magic that humans have been perfecting for millennia. When you write, you are always *responding to* the views of others, whether they are political opponents, cultural critics, close friends, scholars from the past or present, or voices from popular culture. To "respond to" others doesn't always, or even usually, mean "fight." Your own views might:

1. coincide with well-established views, but rest on new support;
2. highlight an omission in the current critical debate;
3. provide new evidence that revises a popular belief;
4. provide an alternative explanation to an accepted view;
5. summarize the body of existing literature in a helpful way;
6. build a new argument that draws on the structure and content of existing arguments.

You get the point: a critical debate usually contains a wide range of complex relationships between popular views, some radically opposed, others nearly identical. The challenge you need to undertake in critical thinking and effective writing is to find your place within the conversation.

Many critical debates devolve into bizarre and unproductive fights, but they shouldn't. So, before we talk about identifying particular debates in various fields, let's establish some rules. There is a bad trend in academic writing, where authors ruthlessly attack each other's personalities and minor faults because they disagree. Don't do this. Respect your interlocutors (those involved in the discussion) as you would like to be respected, even if you find the opposing views less than respectable. You are welcome to contest the views of others in a critical debate, but the point of a debate is never to fight, but rather to convince.

You should also be aware of a serious temptation in critical thinking to take on extreme views. The desire to make "your own mark" in thinking and writing can lead you—and has occasionally led us—to radical views that stand in perfect contrast to other views, just for the sake of being contrarian. There is nothing wrong with having a view antithetical to a popular view, but it should be supported by good evidence. This trend toward extreme views is even more appealing when you discover other writers making a similar dramatic move. The Harvard political scientist Cass Sunstein wrote, "When like-minded people get together, they often end up thinking a more extreme version of what they thought before they started to talk to one another."[1] Resist the allure of black and white thinking. It may feel like you are being edgy in an interesting way, or perfectly original, but the point of thinking and writing isn't usually to be edgy or perfectly original, but rather helpful.

In a recent interview for *Thinking through Writing*, author and philosophy professor Clancy Martin put a point on it for us: "Guys," he paused for a second, "the point of right thinking is not to show off, but to make a contribution, in other words, to help." When you enter a particular field of academic study, professional expertise, or cultural critique—when you encounter a critical debate and decide to enter—it is always good to remember Clancy's words.

How to Identify a Debate in a Field

When you start to write about anything—and we mean anything—it is best to figure out first what has already been written about it. That is the lesson from the last section, but it is, in many cases, easier said than done. Why? Because critical debates often arise in academic fields of study that are very difficult to understand. Since the rise of the modern university in the middle of the nineteenth century, scholar-teacher-writers (more commonly known as professors) have dedicated their lives to developing literature specific to their academic field. If you are an anthropology professor, you are probably not going to write

---

1. Cass R. Sunstein, *On Rumor: How Falsehoods Spread, Why We Believe Them, and What Can Be Done* (Princeton, NJ: Princeton University Press, 2014), 6.

articles in computer science. Each discipline—art history, political science, name your favorite—has its own jargon (specialized lingo) and conventions for debate. As you become more familiar with a particular field of study, you will be able to translate this jargon into meaningful ideas, but way before that you will need to be able to identify specific debates in your field. How?

Debates are about issues and involve people, like you and me, who assume particular viewpoints. We will talk about the different aspects of the viewpoints in a second, but for now, you can think about it as an intellectual wrestling position that readies a writer to grapple with an idea in a specific way. Take the idea of a historical event: "African American slavery in the United States in the 1850s." This issue has always elicited critical debate. Obviously, the two sides were clearly drawn in the lead-up to the American Civil War—abolitionism vs. slave holders— and thinkers went to their inkstands to defend their respective beliefs regarding a single, very important question: "Is slavery justified? Why or why not?" Now, without knowing anything about the actual debate that raged between 1830 and 1870 over the issue of slavery in America, you can probably anticipate the arguments that were made. And this is the first step in identifying a critical debate in a field of study: put a contentious issue at the center of your mental sights and anticipate the questions that might emerge. You are, in effect, identifying problems or questions that have prompted, or could prompt, a wide range of plausible answers. Try a similar process on the idea of slavery, but imagine what writers might argue about the historical event *today*. Take a second. Think about it. We will burn a little bit of time as your mind whirs and spins.

Now, think along with us. From the vantage point of the present day, the issue of slavery still presents a number of historical and sociological questions that invite critical debate.

1. What were the central causes of the institution of slavery?
2. When exactly did slavery start and end in the United States?
3. What implications has slavery had on African Americans living in the United States today?
4. What should be done by the US government regarding the historical occurrence of slavery in a nation premised on freedom?

All of these questions could be—and, in fact, are—the bases of arguments that have filled thousands of written pages in newspapers, magazines, academic books, court opinions, and textbooks. By anticipating the questions that might surround a topic, you are getting a sense of where and how you may contribute to the topic in a meaningful way. But you are also teaching yourself to understand the shape and landscape of a critical debate that is probably already underway.

How to Get to Know the Players in a Critical Debate

When you set your sights on a particular critical debate, you are bound to hear a wide array of different perspectives. Describing these perspectives—at least to yourself—will help you enter the debate fluidly and effectively. Think of this as going to a dinner party or night club and standing at edge of the crowd, looking in. Before you enter the room, you will want to get your best "read" of the players so that you can contribute to the scene in your own unique way, whether it be to complement, criticize, clarify, or expand on a certain part of the scene.

Every player in a critical debate is a speaker, and every speaker expresses themselves in what is known as a "rhetorical situation." The aspects of the rhetorical situation provide the categories for understanding the players—just as mass, color, texture, volume, and so on provide the categories for understanding a physical object. So, what are the aspects of the rhetorical situation? So glad you asked: there are five.

1. When you observe the players (writers) in a rhetorical situation (debate), you will notice that they are always talking to someone or a group of people. This is the *audience* of a given rhetorical situation. You will come to understand the crucial importance of understanding your audience in a moment, but for now let's just say that without an audience, your writing is like a tree falling in a desolate forest: it doesn't make much of a sound.

2. The selection of an audience will depend in large part on the *topic* of the rhetorical situation, or the issue around which a debate centers.

3. Every writer has—or should have—a definite *purpose* in relation to the topic at hand, a reason why he, she, or they are attempting to communicate. Is your purpose to convince, motivate, elucidate, demonstrate, test, question, or something else?

4. The purpose of communicating will often determine the *genre* of the rhetorical situation, the type of writing that needs to be undertaken to achieve a given objective. If you want to woo a heart, you might want the genre of poetry. If you want to urge social change, the manifesto may be your genre.

5. Just as friends and classmates have unique personalities, every writer takes on a particular *stance* in regard to a topic. This isn't exactly the same as saying

that each writer undertakes a specific purpose, but rather observing that writers can be more or less confrontational, educational, assuaging, funny, somber, ironic, inquisitive, or any other stance that suits them. Stance refers to your outlook or position in relation to the topic.

Getting to know the players in a critical debate by identifying the various aspects of the rhetorical situations found therein is a good start at reading critically. Reading critically, at the most basic level, is reading in order to carefully

---

Get to Work

ASPECTS OF THE RHETORICAL SITUATION: SOJOURNER TRUTH'S "AIN'T I A WOMAN?"

Read the powerful speech of Sojourner Truth given at the Ohio Women's Rights Convention in May of 1851, on behalf of Black women in first-wave feminism. This speech was later titled "Ain't I a Woman?" Identify the audience, topic, purpose, genre, and stance from the lines from the speech.

May I say a few words? I want to say a few words about this matter.

I am a woman's rights. I have as much muscle as any man, and can do as much work as any man. I have plowed and reaped and husked and chopped and mowed, and can any man do more than that? I have heard much about the sexes being equal; I can carry as much as any man, and can eat as much too, if I can get it. I am as strong as any man that is now. As for intellect, all I can say is, if women have a pint and man a quart—why can't she have her little pint full?

You need not be afraid to give us our rights for fear we will take too much, for we cant take more than our pint'll hold. The poor men seem to be all in confusion, and dont know what to do. Why children, if you have woman's rights, give it to her and you will feel better. You will have your own rights, and they wont be so much trouble.

I cant read, but I can hear. I have heard the bible and have learned that Eve caused man to sin. Well if woman upset the world, do give her a chance to set it right side up again. The Lady has spoken about Jesus, how he never spurned woman from him, and she was right. When Lazarus died, Mary and Martha came to him with faith and love and besought him to raise their brother. And Jesus wept—and Lazarus came forth. And how came Jesus into the world? Through God who created him and woman who bore him. Man, where is your part? But the women are coming up blessed be God and a few of the men are coming up with them. But man is in a tight place, the poor slave is on him, woman is coming on him, and he is surely between-a hawk and a buzzard.[1]

1. Sojourner Truth (Isabella Baumfree), Ohio Women's Rights Convention speech as transcribed by Marius Robinson, *Anti-slavery Bugle*, June 21, 1851, sourced in *Chronicling America: Historic American Newspapers*, Library of Congress, https://chroniclingamerica.loc.gov/lccn/sn83035487/1851-06-21/ed-1/seq-4/.

examine the "what, why, and how" of a piece of writing. We think that the framework of the rhetorical situation is a helpful one to get you started.

Find Your Niche

In 1851, Sojourner Truth inserted herself into the critical debate surrounding slavery in the United States. And she did so successfully, significantly, momentously, because she carved out a niche in the discussion. A niche is an environmental space in which a particular animal species can fit itself and thrive. No other animal can occupy the niche as effectively, at least for the time being. Think of Darwin's finches in the Galapagos with their specialized beaks designed to crack nuts—and therefore survive—in a specific environment. Now, speaker-writers find their niche when they find a distinct debating space, if you will, to make a particular type of argument. Many years ago, there was a Smokey the Bear commercial for fire prevention in which he said to a viewer, "Only YOU can prevent forest fires." ONLY you can occupy your rhetorical niche—you just have to find it. Now you might say to yourself, "Oh great, they are telling me just to be original. And that is basically impossible; so much has been said already."

Well, take heart: think about "Ain't I a Woman?" Nothing is new under the sun, but that does not mean we are stuck forever in the past. The above argument is not compelling because it is new (the appeal to human rights and equal capabilities was made repeatedly through the early nineteenth century on behalf of the oppressed), but rather because Sojourner Truth placed the arguments in a fresh order, adopted a compelling first-person stance, and redeployed time-tested philosophical argument on behalf of a population not yet largely heard from (Black women). She went after an argument that she thought was true, and either intentionally or inadvertently found arguments and support that had been expressed in other contexts. Originality is not a matter of creating something out of thin air, but rather creating a new order or framework from already existing materials.

Recently we asked the University of Texas at Austin philosopher Galen Strawson how he thinks about entering a critical debate while aiming for something genuinely new. He responded,

[1] I remember Pascal. "Let no one say that I have said nothing new: the organization of the subject matter is new. When we play tennis, we both play with the same ball, but one of us places it better." This is fundamental. It's why introductions to philosophy can be important contributions to the subject. [2] I remember P. F. Strawson: "metaphysics ... has constantly to be done over again." [3] I never think about originality. I try extremely hard to say what I think is true, and am moved when I find old expressions of the same or similar ideas.

So, try hard to say something that is true in relation to a topic, that could change the minds of a given audience, and realize that there are probably other thinkers who have made closely related arguments. It will, then, become your responsibility to search these arguments out.

A final word about finding your niche. In the words of Ralph Waldo Emerson, "Trust thyself, every heart vibrates to that iron string."[2] Trust that you have a contribution to make, that you can bring some of what marketers and corporate executives call "value add" to a critical debate. John's eleven-year-old daughter, Becca, was asked to write about taxis for a school essay. She decided to write about Ubers, or ride-sharing. But everyone writes about ride-sharing. So Becca, from her experiences on the school bus, wrote an essay about how ride-sharing could replace school transit and eliminate bullying. That was her angle; that was the unique rhetorical niche that she could occupy. Part of finding your niche is also a matter of finding, or better knowing, yourself. Get to it.

---

2. Ralph Waldo Emerson, *Self-Reliance and Other Essays* (Mineola, NY: Dover, 1993), 20.

CLOSE READING

Every teacher and most students have at least the vague sense that thinking and writing are inextricably linked to reading. This sense is not at all misguided. But let's clarify and unpack the intuition. When you read, when you read anything, your eyes or hands course over a surface filled with symbols representing another person's thoughts. They could be thoughts about a fictional scene or conversation, or poetic thoughts conveyed in meter and rhyme, or thoughts about a particular subject, or thoughts about other people's thoughts. Sometimes when you read, you will be transported by these symbols to another place and time; in this case, you don't think about the piece of fiction or history, but rather merely enjoy the immersive feeling of reading. But there are other times, and many times in college, when you will be asked to think about a piece of writing rather than allowing it to simply envelop you. You, in turn, will be asked to write out your thoughts about the piece of writing, so that other thinkers can read them.

What should writers read and why? There are several well-worn answers, none of which are totally wrong. The answers boil down: read the good; read the bad; and read all of it. Ben Jonson, the famous English critic, once claimed, "For a man to write well, there are required three necessaries: to read the best authors, observe the best speakers, and much exercise of his own style."[3] That's probably true, but reading amazing work is usually daunting and disheartening, a fact that the twentieth-century American writer Edward Albee reflects upon in his following suggestion regarding reading:

---

3. Ben Jonson, *Timber, or Discoveries Made Upon Men and Matter*, ed. Felix E. Schelling (Boston: Ginn & Company, 1892), 57.

If you are going to learn from other writers don't only read the great ones, because if you do that you'll get so filled with despair and the fear that you'll never be able to do anywhere near as well as they did that, you'll stop writing. I recommend that you read a lot of bad stuff, too. It's very encouraging. "Hey, I can do so much better than this." Read the great stuff but read the stuff that isn't so great, too. Great stuff is very discouraging.[4]

One might find their way between these extreme positions and just read mediocre stuff. But there's a third view. As William Faulkner advised, "Read everything—trash, classics, good and bad, and see how they do it. Just like a carpenter who works as an apprentice and studies the master. Read! You'll absorb it. Then write. If it is good, you'll find out."[5]

Close Reading and the "Text"

A close reading is one that allows the reader to uncover some insight or inner meaning of a text. A close reading begins in observing or experiencing the details, keywords, facts, and patterns of a given text. After you have done this—which is not easy but not the most challenging task in the world—you have to turn to the second stage of close reading, which involves interpreting or making sense of your observations. This is not unlike a biologist who conducts field experiments: first the observations are made, and then tentative conclusions are reached by interpreting

---

4. Quoted in Jon Winokur, comp., *Advice to Writers* (New York: Pantheon, 1999), 141.

5. James B. Meriwether and Michael Millgate, eds., *Lion in the Garden: Interviews with William Faulkner, 1926–1962* (Lincoln: University of Nebraska Press, 1980), 55.

the facts at hand. Every close reading should have the ability to yield a unique interpretation of a text, whether the reading is just a paragraph, a chapter, a series of vignettes, or the work on the whole.

But what do those observations in close reading provide for us? How should we interpret them? Well, we want to take all these bits of info here and there, the stuff that caught our attention, and we want to make something out of them, something like, let's say, an artwork, but an artwork of thinking. A case for something. A conclusion about a specific text.

A "text" we often think about as a book, or magazine article, or formal academic journal article. But a text is really anything that can convey meaning to an observer, and that means that the word "text" can be applied to a whole raft of other forms of expression: songs, poems, movies, political cartoons, graffiti, Instagram images, anything that creates the fertile space for interpretation. Most of your own writing will be prompted by an examination of a variety of texts, so we have to come up with a method of close reading to reveal their inner meaning.

Approaching Texts

When we read a text "closely," we must leave all our habits of everyday reading at the door. We spend plenty of our lives staring at screens, and when we read materials online, our reading attention span is—let's be honest—pretty pathetic. If an article doesn't catch our attention immediately, we are gone before you can spell G-O-N-E. Sixteen seconds is the average read time for most articles that show up on your screen. You will have to multiply that by one hundred in order to get through fifteen pages of Melville's *Moby Dick* or eleven pages of Plato's *Republic*. That makes it sound worse than it actually is: about twenty-six minutes.

The point is that close reading forces you to slow down, to become a different sort of reader—in a way, a different sort of person.

Yes, a different sort of person. Many students do not believe that they can do original research on texts, but everyone who practices close reading will attest that this simply is not true. As a student, it is not enough simply to "get by" in class with dull and unoriginal understandings of the text. The close reader will have the skills to investigate the richness and complexity of a text. And when the investigation is complete, a proficient close reader can situate their original interpretation in the growing conversation of a critical debate and be proud of their contribution.

Close reading is not about finding obvious information as quickly as possible, but rather discovering a buried but important meaning in a text that does not easily reveal itself. Online reading is like metal detecting in a construction site: you can get a lot of pretty worthless stuff very quickly. Close reading is like panning for gold: slow yet rewarding for those who have the patience. In case you need more incentive to learn how to close read: every single college class in the humanities and social sciences will require you to master it (if you want to get an A) as will the exams for law school and graduate school.

Methods of Close Reading

We've addressed the "whys" of close reading, why you might want to spend the time to explore the inner meaning of a text, so it is time to face the "how." The first step in close reading is to go find a pencil. Not a pen, mind you, and certainly *never*, ever a highlighter. We both used to love highlighters. Like really adore them. We would highlight everything, from the beginning to the end of an article, from the very first word of a textbook to the very last. We prided ourselves on our highlighter skills like two high-lighter samurais. This sounds stupid because it was stupid. *Don't be a highlighter samurai.* You will end up high-lighting too much, which will make all your markings more or less meaningless. So, grab a pencil, and do the following. *Oh wait, you say that you read things on the computer and mark things up with the highlighter function?* Well, not anymore. Print out your readings and go get a pencil. And prepare to read something three times, for three different purposes.

1. Start your close reading by putting on your prover-bial reading glasses. What you are looking for in this first pass are key terms, terms that are repeated, terms that are confusing, terms that seem out of place or particularly important to the meaning of the text. Circle or underline them. You have begun to annotate, which means marking things out in the text, and have joined the honor society of scholars who rely on annotation as the springboard for their own writing.

2. Next you want to find what we like to describe to students as a magnifying glass, a conceptual tool for focusing in on particular sections of the text to expose the possible relationship between these sections and others, but also to try to figure out, Sherlock Holmes-style, the *intent* of an author through their use of form and style. The words that come out of a detective's mouth when they use a magnifying glass usually begin with "how" or "why"—and this is a clue about how to make this second step in close reading. You can hear the detective: Why is the candlestick covered with horse hair and blood? How did this horse hair come to be in the library next to this hapless victim? And you can hear the close reader: Why did

Shakespeare use the image of a skull in Hamlet? How does the dialogue surrounding the skull—the famous "to be, or not to be?" soliloquy—serve to foreshadow the rest of the play?

When you use your magnifying glass in close reading, you are no longer simply observing keywords and terms. Look at how a text works. This is a reading for what is called craft or structure and is meant to evaluate author decisions about word choice, organization, and purpose. Here you are asking questions and making guesses about the inner meanings of words, phrases, sentences, and paragraphs. You will need to write out these questions and tentative answers in the margins of your texts, the beginnings of reading notes that we will discuss in a moment.

3. Finally, you will need to employ a metaphorical telescope, a way of reading that tries to situate a part, or the whole, of a text in its wider literary context. To do this, you think to yourself, "Have I read anything, or do I know anything, that is adjacently related to this piece of writing? Is there something that I would like to know about the time in which it was written, about the author or original audience? Or about the books and authors that challenge the view expressed in this text?" You will want to ask, and write out, different questions in this final stage of close reading. Make sure that you tether (or tie closely) your questions to specific passages and make that clear by writing your marginal notes next to given passages, circling parts of the text and drawing arrows or signposts to the question that is related.

MIT professor of philosophy Kieran Setiya recently summed up his approach to critical reading in the following way,

Get to Work

"THE HILL WE CLIMB" (EXCERPT) BY AMANDA GORMAN

Please do a close reading of this excerpt from Amanda Gorman's inaugural poem, "The Hill We Climb." In the process, please follow the numbered prompts below the poem to guide you.

The Hill We Climb
Amanda Gorman

When day comes, we ask ourselves, where can we find
    light in this never-ending shade?
The loss we carry. A sea we must wade.
We braved the belly of the beast.
We've learned that quiet isn't always peace, and the norms
    and notions of what "just" is isn't always justice.
And yet the dawn is ours before we knew it.
Somehow we do it.
Somehow we weathered and witnessed a nation that isn't
    broken, but simply unfinished.
We, the successors of a country and a time where a skinny
    Black girl descended from slaves and raised by a sin-
    gle mother can dream of becoming president, only to
    find herself reciting for one.
And, yes, we are far from polished, far from pristine, but
    that doesn't mean we are striving to form a union that
    is perfect.
We are striving to forge our union with purpose.
To compose a country committed to all cultures, colors,
    characters and conditions of man.
And so we lift our gaze, not to what stands between us,
    but what stands before us.
We close the divide because we know to put our future first,
    we must first put our differences aside.

> We lay down our arms so we can reach out our arms to
>   one another.
> We seek harm to none and harmony for all.
> Let the globe, if nothing else, say this is true.
> That even as we grieved, we grew.
> That even as we hurt, we hoped.
> That even as we tired, we tried.
> That we'll forever be tied together, victorious.
> Not because we will never again know defeat, but because
>   we will never again sow division.[1]

1. Please underline key terms from the poem and connect key terms that are related. Mark repetitions or similarities as well as contrasting terms.
2. What does the poem mean? Underline the lines and phrases that give the clearest sense of the poem's most important meaning. In the margins, write in your own words what this meaning might be.
3. Who is the audience of the poem? Circle the key terms that reveal the audience and write about the audience in the margins of the text.
4. Given the history of "We the people . . ." from the Declaration of Independence, how is Gorman's repeated use of "we" interesting or meaningful?
5. In the formation of the United States, the 1630 sermon of John Winthrop, later called the Sermon of a City on a Hill, formed the basis of political mindset of many Americans who claimed that the United States was to hold a prime place in the political but also cultural and moral order. How does Gorman's poem relate to this idea? Mark and annotate places in the poem that touch on this idea.

---

1. Amanda Gorman, *The Hill We Climb: An Inaugural Poem for the Country* (New York: Viking, 2021), 11–18. Copyright © 2021 by Amanda Gorman. Used by permission of the author.

which seems to reflect many of the above intellectual moves. He said to us,

> My first time reading an article, especially on a subject I don't know much about, I find myself believing everything it says. I have no critical perspective. It's only on a second take that I gain some distance, and I often do that by pretending that I hold a contrary view. Now that I know what the article says, in outline, I imagine being an incredulous reader, not the gullible sap I was. Whatever I end up thinking, I gain a sharper sense of the limitations of the article and of the inner logic of a view that may or may not be my own.

Your "glasses reading" begins by seeing a text clearly. Your magnifying glass and telescope challenge a text to reveal its inner logic, mysteries, and tensions.

Avoiding Close Reading Frustration

Close reading is a skill that is developed over time, usually in the last years of high school or at the outset of college. Many young students think that they are close reading and making effective annotations when they are really just providing a summary of the text. This is not their fault: many English classes encourage a "book report" style of teaching, which does little to prepare students to write compelling essays. Summaries, or shorthand descriptions of the pivotal moves in a text, are useful in certain cases, but they should not be the sole (or even primary) objective of a close reading. Think about it this way: your close reading should reveal something secret, hidden, special—especially important but easily overlooked. The output of a close reading should not be something that you could look up on SparkNotes or an online essay depository. The outcome of *your* close reading is a documentation of *your* thoughts about a given text. So, in your annotations, avoid summary.

When you are undertaking a close reading and begin to annotate, take care that the space in the margins of the text does not restrict your thought. In other words, you need to find a notebook to use for all the texts that you work through, or you need to devise a system that uses space efficiently so that you can develop what are called "reading notes." These notes should direct you back to the text by page number and section and then capture your thoughts and questions about that passage. As you read, you can also follow the example of many writers from the past in making your own index at the back of the book (there are usually a few blank pages at the end, which are perfectly fitted for this purpose). To make your own index, you write keywords, concepts, or phrases from the text in the back of the book and then the pages where you find those words. This will help you move quickly to reorient yourself to a text should you choose to do more work on it in the future.

Finally, remember that your notes do not need to capture one single interpretation that is the "correct take" on a text, or the interpretation that is most often given, or the one that your teacher wants you to grasp. There is no such thing as a single definitive interpretation of a rich text. There are many meaningful interpretations that need to be defended as adequately as possible. That will become your job. This being said, remember that the interpretations of the text are not just "up to you" in the sense of being whatever your heart desires. In developing an interpretation of a text, like a scientist developing a theory to explain a set of data, you must consider and account for observations that another person could make, and conclusions that another thinker could reasonably infer.

ANALYTIC QUESTIONS

The single hardest part of thinking through writing is also the most important: you have to ask the right questions. This should come as no huge surprise since one of the toughest and most vital parts of life is knowing when to ask what questions: "How do I make better friends?" "Why is this the right house for me?" "How will I survive this disease?" "Will you marry me?" You might think that answers and claims are more substantial or significant than questions, but without the right question, you will never, ever, come to the right answer. The question is always primary. Doing a close reading of a text is always a warm-up for asking a number of very good questions, questions that will motivate your own writing. You will learn in the next section that effective writing reflects an author's attempt to answer great questions for themselves.

In terms of close reading, we have suggested writing questions in the margins of the text, questions that you would like to answer for yourself, questions that you would like to ask the author if you had the chance, questions that you would share with a fellow intellectual traveler. In this section, we will talk a little bit about which sort of questions are the best to drive an essay forward. These are known as analytic questions. You probably already have a sense of what it is to analyze a topic (you do it all the time in reading the news or evaluating a friend's take on her favorite band), but we would like to get clearer about what it means in reading and writing.

Writing Prompts

Most of us grow up writing for our teachers. We sat through a literature or history class, where we were given a mountain of texts to read. At the end of the class, our teacher assigned a series of writing "prompts," which invited us to write about Lincoln or Hamilton or Harry Potter, or whatever. "Discuss the relationship between Hamilton and Burr." "Discuss the meaning of the 'Golden Snitch' in the *Sorcerer's Stone*." Unfortunately, we often don't know where to start, and so we assume that the task is to figure out what our teacher wants us to say. This is the singularly wrong way to approach a writing assignment. Every good teacher wants two things from their students:

1. Teachers want their students to have grappled carefully with the text and to show, in some way, what this investigation has meant to them. Of course, this means that a student has to show the teacher that they understand some of the details and finer points of the actual text. But a good teacher wants something more for and from their pupils.

2. They want to see, in the course of a student essay, the attempt to make an original interpretation. In other words, they would like to see students organize their thoughts into novel claims about the text at hand. This is the creative moment in all of academic writing—why being a teacher and being a student can be so exciting—and an aspect of thinking and writing that is never to be downplayed.

Let us say a word about essay "prompts." A prompt can take many different forms in many different classes. Frequently teachers will ask you to "discuss" a topic, as in the cases above. This is not an invitation to speak generally around a subject or to express a few loosely related opinions. Don't be fooled: it is a rather firm suggestion to pose a specific question about the subject and then support an answer to the question over the course of an essay.

Some teachers will give a little more direction in prompts, and it is wise to heed it. Keep an eye out for keywords in essay prompts that give clues about what sort of essay will be expected. If you see words like "evaluate," "critique," and "assess," you will know that your professor is looking for you to interpret a section of text or a particular topic. If you see "compare" and "contrast," they are looking for you to establish and argue for a novel relation between two things, characters, or texts on the whole.

Analysis vs. Synthesis

Writing prompts prompt us to write, but let us first be prompted to think. There are two primary ways that humans think about their world: through what is known as analysis and synthesis. Analysis is a mode of sorting out the world by taking it apart and thinking hard about its different parts that make up the whole. Analysis means breaking a subject down and then piecing it together to see how it works.

When he was twelve, John wanted to know how his window air conditioner worked. So he analyzed it. He got a screwdriver and pliers and took it apart, and laid all of the parts out on his bedroom floor. Of course, this did not reveal the inner mystery of the air conditioner until his mother commanded that he put it back together. At that point, he was forced to undertake the (almost impossible) task of figuring out the relationship between all the disparate parts—this compressor is fitted to this circuit board, which is attached to this framework—which took him three months. At the end of three months, it still didn't work, so the analysis was only partially successful. Now, analysis doesn't usually have to be this painful, but it is the process of identifying different aspects of a topic, pulling them apart in order to understand them distinctively, and then in relationship.

Where do we find analysis? Everywhere. An anatomical drawing of the head, revealing its various bones and

muscles and nerves, showing how everything works together, is a demonstration of analysis. An engineering blueprint of a wind turbine, examining its motors and fans, is
the product of analysis. Any sort of map that shows the
relationship between major roads, county byways, gas sta-
tions, and malls—again, a result of analysis. The close reading that you do with texts, sets you up to conduct analysis
by highlighting certain features of the text, or concentrat-
ing on only certain passages. The trick is to sort through
your observations and then put them together in original
ways, to reveal something about the whole. As you will see,
the questions that we ask about a text often perform the
task of analysis by interrogating specific aspects or sections of your readings.

Now, synthesis is the second, and equally important,
way of thinking through the world at large. Instead of
breaking a topic down in order to understand it by way
of its different parts, synthesis proceeds by bringing a
whole topic or text into relationship with other related
topics or texts. You can think about this as grasping something by way of acknowledging and thinking about its context. How do you understand your friends? Is it by way of
scrutinizing specific things they say or do, breaking down
their every move? Well, sometimes—and this would be in
the act of analysis. But there is another way.

Try to think about your friends in terms of their history,
in terms of their loved ones, their other friends, their passions, and the wider world they occupy. This is an attempt
to think about your friends synthetically, by way of the
relationship that they, on the whole, hold to a broader
context. Great writers work both analytically and synthetically, cutting apart a topic to reveal something that
deserves attention, while at the same time setting the
topic in a revealing relationship to its surroundings. That
being said, let's start with the analysis of a text, since it is

self-contained, meaning that no external knowledge, beyond the text itself, is required in analysis.

Crafting an Analytic Question

The questions you develop in your close reading that you
pose to yourself, the author, or a fellow reader, will be the
sort of questions that set textual analysis in good position.
These analytic questions ask about specific parts, aspects,
and relationships in a text, in order to expose something
significant or meaningful about the text as a whole. These
questions—typically "how" or "why" questions—do not
have a single, simple answer. They are never, ever answered
by a mere "yes" or "no." Instead, they open a conversation
between various interpretations and invite a variety of
possible, plausible answers. We asked Columbia University psychologist Scott Barry Kaufman what makes for a
good question. His answer seems spot on to us:

> Good questions are those that lead naturally to even
> better questions. You know that's happening when
> you are stimulated by a question, are thinking more
> deeply about it than you ever have before, and are
> motivated to explore it from multiple angles. There
> is this tendency to focus on the answer immediately,
> but often a pause and reframing of a question can
> lead to more interesting discoveries. I try to look for
> open-ended questions that divergently suggest mul-
> tiple possible answers than those that convergently
> lead to expectations of a single correct answer.

With Kaufman's comment in mind, let us propose six cardinal virtues of great analytic questions:

1. *They have a laser focus.* Great essays are usually not
   broad, superficial treatments of a major topic, but

rather a deep dive into one specific aspect of a topic that reveals something new about the whole.

2. *They don't have simple "yes or no" answers.* "Yes or no" answers make for very short essays, in which an audience is either forced to agree or strictly disagree in uninteresting ways.

3. *They invite interpretation.* The questions that you pose should be the first step in developing a novel interpretation or "take" on a text.

4. *They invite controversy.* You want to jump into an essay and make an argument that an audience will potentially take issue with. This is not for the sake of argument per se, but because you want to spend your writing life exploring questions that are interesting and have yet to be resolved or answered.

5. *They can be answered by the text itself.* Make sure that the question you pick sets the stage for an answer that can be supported by features of the text you are examining.

6. *They are motivating to an audience.* Every author needs to ask themselves the "So what?" question. You need to ask why and how an audience might care about the questions that you are posing.

There is a tendency to think that broad or general questions are potentially the most interesting. They appeal to the broadest audience, right? Not exactly. Broad questions are often a sign of a reader's laziness, an indication that one has not taken the task of close reading seriously. When you close in on the text, you read particular passages and examine specific ideas and scenes, and this necessarily narrows your focus on a unique facet of a broader topic. As students, we were often taught by instructors: "Stick to the text!" This meant that we were to examine the inner meaning of the text, by way of an analysis of its key features and formal elements.

Honing an Analytic Question

In our experience, the trick to finding a great analytic question is honing and refining not-so-great ones. Here are a few tips on how to do that:

1. *Interrogate a key concept.* When you read Gorman's "The Hill We Climb," perhaps you underlined the key term "hope," and in the margin you wrote, "How does hope work in the poem?" This is a nice beginning. Let's make it better. You can interrogate (or ask about) the concept of hope by amending the question: "Is hope used in a positive, negative, neutral, or ambiguous way?" This will allow you to think carefully about the exact definition of hope that is at play for Gorman, a definition that she never makes explicit, but one that you can articulate in the course of an essay.

2. *Make distinctions in a text (or slice-and-dice the text).* Let's say you are reviewing your reading notes for a class on Shakespeare and you find the following question: "How does humor accompany tragedy in Shakespeare?" Shakespeare wrote thirty-six plays. So, you must pick one, or at least limit the investigation to two or three illustrative soliloquies from different plays. Then the question might be amended: "How do three central soliloquies from *Othello*, *Hamlet*, and *Macbeth* reveal the relationship between tragedy and humor?" A similar sort of move could be made with Gorman's poem, in which you focus on moments of description in the poem and ask how they stand against hope: "How does hope emerge as the motivation for the victories that Gorman describes in her poem?" In honing the question in this fashion, you have sliced and diced the poem, pulling out moments describing partial victories and then setting them in relation to a particular kind of hope.

3. *Defy expectations.* Some of the best questions are those that expose and counteract popular or common ways of thinking about a text or about the world. So be comfortable asking questions that defy expectations. You will have to write a little more into your questions, but this is fine. Let's see how it works on the Gorman question: "How does hope stand in relation to the partial victories that Gorman describes in her poem? Is this sort of hope the motivation or the outcome of striving for, and persisting for, unfulfilled yet ideal goals?" Hope is usually the force that drives one into action, but perhaps hope is the byproduct of partial successes of African Americans in the United States since the nation's inception.

One thing should become clear in these tips for analytic question formation: in each case, the process of honing a question often involves making the question *longer*. Of course, making a question longer (including more words) will not necessarily help produce good questions, but, as a rule, more words are needed to make more specific questions that identify the exact scope that interests you.

This discussion of analysis and analytic questions is the essential preparation for what is taken as the keystone of many College Writing courses: the formation of a meaningful thesis. That is where we are headed next.

THESIS FORMATION

In junior high school, most English teachers tell their students, in no uncertain terms, that an academic essay must be centered around a particular thesis, and a thesis is the main point, or claim, or argument that an author wants to make. Unfortunately, many things we learn in junior high are simplified, making them somewhat unhelpful later in adult life.

A thesis is not, at its essence, a claim, or point, or an argument. It is, at its essence, an answer to a question. The question is the *sine qua non* (the "without which not") of a thesis. Why is this a better way to think of a thesis? It places wonder, confusion, perplexity—the feelings of having a real problem—at the very heart of your writing. The point of writing is to resolve, amplify, or explain these feelings. Thinking of a thesis as an answer to a question builds in the motivation for your paper or essay. The question, that stimulating doubt that arose in your reading or observing, is the reason to write an essay and the reason for someone to read it.

Defining a Strong Thesis

A strong thesis, therefore, is the answer to a strong analytic question. It should be an answer that you would like to explore and ultimately support through research and argumentation. So, the thesis should be able to be expressed in an "I will argue X" statement, even if it is developed in a different way. In many scholarly papers, you will actually see authors express their theses in precisely this way: "I will argue," or "we will argue," or "this paper will argue." Your thesis statement will often be found at the outset of an essay in the first or second paragraph of an introduction. This typical placement, which we will discuss at length in the next chapter, is designed to alert a reader of your intentions as an author. You want to convince an audience of something, and that something is expressed in your thesis. After reading your introduction and evaluating your thesis, readers should think to themselves, "Hmm—this author wants to win me over to their way of thinking about X. I am not there yet, but I am open to being convinced. Let's see where this goes." If your reader thinks this to themselves, you have written a strong thesis and have the chance to change their minds about the topic at hand.

A strong thesis must take a stand. This means that you, as a writer, have to assume a definite position on a topic. It is not sufficient to say, "I will argue that the poet Amanda Gorman says many interesting things about hope in her poem 'The Hill We Climb.'" This is not a strong, stand-taking thesis. This is: "I will argue that Gorman's poem, 'The Hill We Climb,'" sets out a very particular idea of hope—bittersweet, realistic, and constructive—which stems from the unique strivings of the African American experience." That is a position that could be defended through evidence from the text, and it is a claim that could stand against other distinct interpretations.

A strong thesis must be debatable. Other points of view need to be readily apparent: don't pick a claim that can be made without friction or contention. Consider these not-so-stellar theses: "I will argue that Amanda Gorman's poetry isn't too bad"; "I will argue that Sojourner Truth is kind of important in American history." These weak claims are hardly debatable. Your thesis must initiate an argument worth making and have a grip on a number of different positions.

A strong thesis must be specific. It should only cover what you are able to argue in your essay, and your thesis should be able to be supported by available evidence. If you pose an "I will argue X" in your thesis, will it be possible for you to do so? Make sure you have narrowed the question and answer (thesis) sufficiently so that they can organize and provide a contained shape of what might be a very short essay. Measure the specificity and complexity of your thesis against the length of the paper or essay that you aim to pull off. This is also to say that you must refine the scope (or the intellectual reach) of a thesis so that it can say something genuinely new and meaningful about a set of observations or insights regarding the text.

A strong thesis telegraphs and foreshadows the structure and message of an essay. Without giving away too much, an effective thesis hints at what will come in the course of your writing. It creates accountability for you, as the writer, and creates expectation for your reader.

A Working Thesis

Defining a strong thesis is much, much easier than actually crafting one. Tough questions, the sort that deserve good answers, are never solved on the first try. That is why most writers employ what is known as a working thesis. A working thesis is the tentative answer to the analytic question that grounds a piece of writing. You revise the working thesis in the course of your research. Let's say you are writing an essay about René Descartes, the French thinker who famously claimed, "I think, therefore I am," and you have jotted down an interesting question in your reading notes: "How do the cultural and historical forces of Descartes's time influence the writing of his *Meditations*?" Nice question. A little too broad and not tightly enough bound to the text, but it is a start. Now, you might propose the following working thesis.

"I will argue that the scientific revolution, the discovery of the New World, and the Protestant Reformation directly influenced Descartes's *Meditations*."

One thing that you will immediately notice is the wordy—overly broad—focus of the thesis. You will want to narrow things down as you move forward on your research, but the point of a working thesis is to get the ball rolling and give you some direction in your research. As you learn more about Descartes and read the *Meditations* more carefully, you discover that the scientific revolution was more important than the other cultural forces expressed above, so you amend your working thesis:

> "I will argue that the scientific revolution, more than other cultural and historical factors, had a major influence on Descartes's writing of the *Meditations*."

This is better, because it is more focused, but one more revision of this working thesis might be made. You discover in reading the *Meditations* that Descartes is trying to combat the skepticism or extreme doubt surrounding the modern sciences. His is an attempt to secure the firmest foundation for the sciences. So, you can make the final revision to the working thesis:

> "I will argue that the scientific revolution, more than other cultural and historical factors, had a major influence on Descartes's writing of the *Meditations*, specifically, setting the stage for Descartes's attempt to establish a foundation for human knowledge that could not be doubted."

We will address argumentation in the coming chapter, but we would like to observe at this point that the revised thesis sets out a very specific task for this author. She will have to first show that other historical factors (like the discovery of the New World) are not as pivotal as the scientific revolution for Descartes, and then she will be forced to identify passages in the *Meditations* that directly relate to skepticism and to the challenges of modern science. While difficult, this is far from impossible, and will make the writing of a compelling paper more than manageable.

What a Thesis Is Not

If you keep the "I will argue" construction in mind, it will be a good way to avoid some very tempting mistakes in developing a thesis. But we should outline some of the common pitfalls anyway—call us neurotic; we don't care. So here are three guidelines on what a thesis is not and can never be.

A thesis is never a description. "I will argue that Socrates meets Euthyphro on the steps of the courthouse in the Platonic dialogue." This is simply a matter of fact and can easily be ascertained in a quick reading of the dialogue. Make sure that your thesis proposes something that can be supported by the text, but something that is not self-evident (or indisputable) in the reading of the text. Try this for an alternative: "By placing the meeting of Socrates and Euthyphro on the steps of the courthouse, Plato indicates that both characters have yet to fully understand the nature of the good, or enter the true meaning of the law, and must stand outside and think critically about morality before entering." This might not be the best thesis, but it puts forward an interpretation of the text that can be tested by the text and the discussion that ensues between the two characters about morality and the law.

A thesis should never include a no-duh list. "I will argue John F. Kennedy was influenced by his family, by his experience in the church, by his education, and by his friends, in early adolescence." Yes, and so was almost every other Catholic kid growing up in the 1930s. This is a "no-duh list" of explanatory factors. Such lists are exhaustive and obvious, and therefore pretty uninteresting; they make no real claim and take no real stand, although you could imagine a textureless essay in which each paragraph or section details a different influencing factor. B-O-R-I-N-G. If you are drawn to list, think about prioritization: which factor is most important? Which is the least important, and why?

A thesis should never be unnecessarily aggressive or congratulatory. "I will argue that Sojourner Truth is the best feminist—ever." Taking a debatable stand is one thing. Being over the top is quite another. Make sure that you are not arguing a broad and emotionally laden point in your thesis. If you find yourself using words like "best," "worst," "evil," "perfect," or "stupid" to paint a topic in broad brushstrokes, take a second look and see if you might be able to refine your thesis. You probably can.

We believe in your powers of thesis formation, and, motivated by our belief, we've set aside a space, a *poetic* space, for you to exercise those powers. Poems are a rich source of meanings, of overtones and undertones, and therefore a rich source for forming theses.

Wrapping Up

Writing usually begins in a certain type of reading: close, careful, critical reading. You can learn how to write and how not to by observing the style and form of other writers. When you read anything, you have the chance to ask questions to yourself, to the author, or to fellow readers about the text, whether it be a comic, a political poster, or a great novel. This is your opportunity to engage in the ancient human practice of analysis, breaking down a subject into its constitutive parts in order to understand the relationship between the parts, and see something new or significant about the whole. Forming analytic questions is the first step in generating worthwhile theses, since a thesis is an answer to one of these types of questions. A thesis is essentially an answer, a proposal that will motivate your

Get to Work

THESIS FORMATION

Imagine you are in a class on comparative literature, religious studies, Middle Eastern thought, or college writing, and you're asked to read and write about the thirteenth-century Sufi Muslim mystic poet Rumi. It could happen . . . really. You are given his poem, which is usually translated as "Unmarked Boxes." Take a minute (actually maybe twenty minutes) and do a close reading of the poem, annotating the poem with an eye toward the topic of suffering, the topic of nature, and the topic of God.

Unmarked Boxes
Jalal al-Din Rumi (1207–73)

Don't grieve. Anything you lose comes round
in another form. The child weaned from mother's milk
now drinks wine and honey mixed.

God's joy moves from unmarked box to unmarked box,
from cell to cell. As rainwater, down into flowerbed.
As roses, up from ground.
Now it looks like a plate of rice and fish,
now a cliff covered with vines,
now a horse being saddled.
It hides within these,
till one day it cracks them open.

Part of the self leaves the body when we sleep
and changes shape. You might say, "Last night
I was a cypress tree, a small bed of tulips,
a field of grapevines." Then the phantasm goes away.
You're back in the room.
I don't want to make anyone fearful.
Hear what's behind what I say.

Tatatumtum tatum tatadum.
There's the light gold of wheat in the sun

and the gold of bread made from that wheat.
I have neither. I'm only talking about them,
as a town in the desert looks up
at stars on a clear night.[1]

1. Write THREE working theses that bear on your annotations in the margins.
2. Choose one of those three theses and refine it, specifically by narrowing the scope of the claims that you are going to make.

---

1. Rumi, *The Essential Rumi*, trans. Coleman Barks (New York: HarperCollins, 1995), 272.

writing and motivate your audience to follow your argument from beginning to end. We often tell students that the point of an essay is to show your reader something that they have never seen before but that they desperately need to. A successful thesis, one that is well-scoped and deep, supportable by the text and debatable, will change a reader's way of seeing the world, or, at the very least, a small part of it. That is the hope.

An essay without a powerful thesis is pointless, boring, uninteresting, or confusing. A thesis without an argument and support is largely powerless. So, we will turn our attention next to the thorny matter of making an argument—for argument's sake.

EXERCISES

1. Find a sentence anywhere in our "Analytic Questions" section and "ask" two questions about that sentence. For example:

   Sentence: "In terms of close reading, we have suggested writing questions in the margins of the text, questions that you would like to answer for your-self, questions that you would like to ask the author if you had the chance, questions that you would share with a fellow intellectual traveler."

Question 1: Who counts as a "fellow intellectual traveler"?

Question 2: What if my questions are so inti-mate that I feel anxious about writing them down?

2. In the "Find Your Niche" subsection, we asked you to "trust that you have a contribution to make." If you don't already possess that trust that you have contributions to make, this thinking and writing exercise can help draw that out. What makes you unique or different from most people? Write down three or four things that make you different from most people—the ways you think, your background, your interests, and so on. Think deeply and broadly about your own lived experiences. Then consider how these differences and experiences may structure how you think about writing topics.

Chapter 2

THINKING THROUGH ARGUMENTS

WHAT IS AN ARGUMENT?

"Don't argue!" Both of our mothers were so very clear about this. What they really meant, however, was "don't fight with your brother."

There is a crucial difference between an argument and a fight. Fighting happens when people have lost the ability or desire to argue effectively. Fighting is the attempt to coerce someone to do something or believe something—by means of force. An argument is an attempt to convince, rather than bully, a person to see things your way. More precisely, an *argument* is a series of statements that are linked in a special logical relationship. Some statements in an argument we call *premises*, and some statements we call *conclusions*. The basic idea is that when we add up our premises, the truth of the conclusion is secured. Your interlocutor (or opponent) might say one thing. And you have to learn to say another to make them change their mind. We asked Mariana Alessandri, associate professor of philosophy at the University of Texas Rio Grande Valley, what she thinks about good, even great, arguments.

A great argument doesn't always sound great. Sometimes it sounds like a drag if it's an ethical argument, or like a bore if it's a purely logical one. But what makes it great is timelessness: a strong argument won't crumble when you start poking at it. A horrible argument, on the other hand, might sound really convincing—it's designed to!—but it falls apart with a little questioning.

There is no other way to evaluate and measure the strength or weakness of a claim, but by cross-examination, by questioning the argument—so question away. If you are having trouble asking good questions about a given argument, it might have less to do with the argument itself and more to do with your relationship to the conclusion. Alessandri explained, "If you like where an argument's going, ask yourself why. And be honest. Would you still agree with its premises if there were nothing in it for you?" We need to be as clear and sincere as possible in expressing and evaluating the statements we make in speech or the written word.

Arguments: Premises, Conclusions, and Inferences

We will start with the basics. When we make an argument, we start with a statement. Any statement. Let's use "Maria is nice" as our statement, and let's ask ourselves if that statement is a premise or a conclusion. Pause and think about it before stampeding to the answer in the next paragraph.

Well, so far, "Maria is nice" is neither a premise nor a conclusion. We haven't located it in an argument yet. It is simply a statement without a home. Happily, we can use "Maria is nice" as a premise or a conclusion. Consider the two arguments below. In argument 1, "Maria is nice" is the premise. In argument 2, "Maria is nice" is the conclusion.

1. Maria is nice, so she probably donates to charity.

2. Maria helps everybody she meets. Maria is nice.

For the record, we can also make "Maria is nice" both a premise and a conclusion:

3. Maria is nice; therefore, Maria is nice.

In argument 1, "Maria is nice" is used to support a conclusion about Maria's charitable donations. In argument 2, we conclude that "Maria is nice" on the basis of her helping everybody she meets. Let's ignore for the moment whether these are good arguments, and just enjoy the fact that "Maria is nice" can fit nicely into any argument as a premise, a conclusion, or both.

Be careful not to confuse the order in which we write our statements with the *logical order* of an argument. In argument 2, "Maria is nice" is the conclusion and comes last, but we can easily rewrite that argument:

2A. Maria is nice. Maria helps everybody she meets.

Like an omnipresent god, conclusions can go anywhere (and so can premises). The challenge is to detect which statements are in the supporting role (premises) and which statements are being supported (conclusions). Sometimes it is not clear what is meant to support what. Writers often throw many statements together, without any particular sense of hierarchy, of what supports what exactly. It is like group therapy: the statements are just mutually supportive. Still, we would like to know how things fit together logically. If we think our statements should be supported, then we need to understand how premises support conclusions. This brings us to the topic of inferences.

INFERENCES

We found a T-shirt on Twitter that read as follows:

There are two types of people in this world: (1) Those who can extrapolate from incomplete data.

Full stop. That is all it says. No second type of person is listed. Yet we can guess the second type of person: "2.

Those who *cannot* extrapolate from incomplete data." But to know about this second type of person, we needed to make an inference. An *inference* is an intellectual step from something to something else. Some inferential steps are small, like baby steps; some are more like vast leaps.

We use logic in order to track our inferences, our intellectual footprints, and avoid stepping from a true proposition onto a steaming pile of false propositions. Said differently, from a true proposition, we want to infer another true proposition, not a false proposition. We want, in other words, the truth to meet us at every step of our thinking.

Consider again some of our Maria examples from above.

3. Maria is nice; therefore, Maria is nice.

As far as inferences go, this is the smallest, safest, least informative inference you can make: the step from something to itself. If "Maria is nice" is a true proposition, then you're guaranteed to step into another true proposition if you simply repeat "Maria is nice." With this inference, there's no worry that you'll start with a true proposition and end with a false proposition.

Let's take a bigger step now.

2. Maria helps everybody she meets. Maria is nice.

What do you think? Should we take the step from the premise "Maria helps everybody she meets" to the conclusion "Maria is nice"? What should we ask ourselves before taking that fateful step? If we want to step from a truth to a truth, then we should ask ourselves something like this question: If the proposition "Maria helps everybody she meets" is true, does its truth guarantee the truth of the conclusion "Maria is nice"? Does the truth of the premise guarantee the truth of the conclusion?

Recall that if "Maria is nice" is true, its truth guarantees the truth of the conclusion "Maria is nice." They're the same proposition, so how could "one" be true and "the other" false? That step is extremely safe. But does such a guarantee of safety occur in argument 2? We don't want to step from a truth into a falsehood, so how should we proceed? Keep that question in mind; we'll come back to it.

Validity and Soundness

VALIDITY

You've probably heard the complaint that something is "invalid," or an approving remark that something is "valid." For logicians, "validity" and "invalidity" are terms of art. In the logician's use of the terms, "validity" and "invalidity" refer to a special relationship between premises and conclusions. Consider these two definitions, which may sound fancy but are simple once you think through them slowly:

> A *deductively valid argument* is an argument in which, if the premises are true, the conclusion cannot be false.

> An *inductively valid argument* is an argument in which, if the premises are true, the conclusion is very likely true.

When we considered arguments about Maria, we wanted to know if our step from a premise to a conclusion was safe. Think of validity as a measure of the safety of our step. The steps in a deductively valid argument are the safest (if the premises are true, the conclusion *cannot* be false). A *deductive argument* (aka "deduction") is a set of premises that aims to make this safest of all steps to a conclusion. Meanwhile, the steps in an inductively valid argument are decently safe, but not 100 percent safe. An *inductive argument* (aka "induction") is a set of premises that aims to make a reasonably safe step to a conclusion.

OK, so how do we know an argument is deductively valid? There is a simple method for determining whether an argument is deductively valid: the counterexample. Let's go back to our Maria argument:

2. Maria helps everybody she meets. Maria is nice.

Now ask yourself this question: Could it be true that "Maria helps everybody she meets" and yet false that "Maria is nice"? In other words (remember our definition of deductive validity), could the premise be true and the conclusion false? If the premise is true, yet the conclusion is false, then our step from the truth of the premise to the truth of conclusion is unsafe.

Consider this possibility: What if Maria is helping everybody she meets only because she thinks it will improve her chances of becoming a top politician, and she plans to become a top politician only so she can enact laws that will financially benefit her at the expense of her electorate? In that case, yes, it's true that Maria helps everybody she meets, yet it's false that Maria is nice. True premise, but false conclusion. This argument is not deductively valid.

It does not make a difference in terms of deductive validity that we *could* tell a story in which it is true that "Maria helps everybody she meets" and simultaneously true that "Maria is nice." Maria may in fact be nice. It doesn't matter, deductively speaking. As long as we find just one counterexample, one way in which the premises can be true and the conclusion false, then we've shown that the argument is not deductively valid.

Deductive validity is the most restrictive degree of validity. We might say that deductive validity, if it were a person, would be the most paranoid about the safety of its steps. Every step *must* be 100 percent safe. There *must* be absolutely *no* possibility of a misstep. God forbid!

Inductive validity, on the other hand, is a freer bird, and a little fuzzier. Inductive validity deals with probabilities and statistical reasoning, among other things. Keeping to our step analogy, we could say that the safety of the final step in an inductively valid argument is above 50 percent, but below 100 percent.

Let's return to Maria:

2. Maria helps everybody she meets. Maria is nice.

Is this argument inductively valid? Well, probably not. Based on the scant information available to us, that "Maria helps everybody she meets," we are probably motivated to assign some probability to the conclusion that "Maria is nice." This just means that it's not *impossible* that Maria is nice, given the premise. That's not much, considering all the possible counterexamples that would show how Maria is not nice, even though she helps everybody she meets. She may also simultaneously hurt everybody she meets. She may intentionally avoid meeting people so she doesn't have to help them. To make this conclusion *inductively valid*, and therefore very likely true, we need more information. Unfortunately, we will likely never get enough information to make the truth of Maria's niceness immune from all possible counterexamples, but that's just the loosey-goosey nature of induction (and life). Inductive reasoning is like building a tentative scientific case for a conclusion; it requires probabilistic guesses and sensitivity to the available evidence. An inductive step is never entirely safe, but one should aim to make it *safe enough*.

SOUNDNESS

Consider the following valid argument: "All monkeys are made of banana pudding. All banana pudding is extremely radioactive. Therefore, all monkeys are extremely radioactive." Imagine some person says that you must accept this argument because it is valid. What do you say to this? Is this person, with their radioactive-banana-pudding-monkey argument, which is indeed deductively valid, correct?

Of course not. The person seems to assume that a deductively valid argument must be accepted as a truth, a kind of absolute checkmate. Far from it. A valid argument is valid, but it is a misstep, a poor inference, to conclude that a valid argument is a *sound* argument, let alone a *good* argument.

A *sound argument* is an argument that is deductively valid and whose premises are actually true. Validity does not require the premises of an argument to be true; it only requires that *if* the premises are true, the conclusion cannot be false. Never forget that subtle difference. Soundness, however, requires the premises to be literally true. So, banana-pudding person is offering us a valid argument, but not a sound argument. Monkeys, we can safely say, are not made of banana pudding, nor is all banana pudding extremely radioactive (just some, perhaps). Don't worry about your banana pudding.

ARGUMENTS FROM ANALOGY AND CAUSE

Arguments from Analogy

Now that we've explored the basics of arguments (premises, conclusions, inferences, validity—both deductive and inductive—and soundness), let's move to two special kinds of argumentation.

The ancient Greek philosopher Epicurus, in his *Letter to Pythocles*, claims that "From terrestrial phenomena it is possible to derive certain indications of what takes place in the heavenly bodies."[1] In other words, from our observations of things here on the earth, we can infer truths about the moon, sun, planets, and stars. Living back there in ancient Athens, Epicurus could hardly employ advanced space telescopes, astronomical spectroscopy, or other contemporary scientific methods for explaining celestial phenomena. Yet explanation needs to start somewhere, and Epicurus's advice, to analogize from terrestrial truths to celestial truths, however shaky it may be, meant appealing to natural phenomena on earth to explain the cosmos, rather than divine choices.

Arguments from analogy, as the example of Epicurus shows, are inductive. The truths of the premises do not 100 percent guarantee the truth of the conclusion, only the likelihood of the conclusion. In the case of arguments by analogy, the likelihood of the conclusion depends on the *similarity* of the things that are being compared.

About sixty years before the birth of Epicurus, Socrates invoked the gods to explain human biology. Socrates's argument is one of the earliest cases of the argument from design, which aims to show that certain complex phenomena, for example, living things like human beings, are best explained by the creative act of an intelligent being.

> Besides these, are there not other contrivances that look like the results of forethought? Thus the eyeballs, being weak, are set behind eyelids, that open like doors when we want to see, and close when we sleep: on the lids grow lashes through which the very winds filter harmlessly: above the eyes is a coping of brows that lets no drop of sweat from the

---

1. Epicurus, *Letter to Pythocles*, in *The Art of Happiness*, trans. George K. Strodach (New York: Penguin Books, 2012), 136.

head hurt them. The ears catch all sounds, but are never choked with them. Again, the incisors of all creatures are adapted for cutting, the molars for receiving food from them and grinding it. And again, the mouth, through which the food they want goes in, is set near the eyes and nostrils; but since what goes out is unpleasant, the ducts through which it passes are turned away and removed as far as possible from the organs of sense. With such signs of forethought in these arrangements, can you doubt whether they are the works of chance or design?[2]

Socrates suggests that certain beneficial bodily features are signs of forethought. These features "look like the results of forethought." Notice that expression "like." Socrates posits a likeness between our bodies and the everyday results of forethought, for example, doors, millstones, and plumbing. If doors, millstones, and plumbing exist due to forethought, then it is *probably* true that bodily features similar to doors, millstones, and plumbing exist due to forethought.

But if similarity is the strength of an argument by analogy, difference is its weakness. Finding relevant differences between items being compared in an analogy will weaken the argument. Yet finding these relevant differences isn't always easy. For example, claiming that doors are made by human doormakers, but that no part of the human body is made by a human doormaker, is not a relevant difference. Socrates is not arguing that our eyelids are literally made by human doormakers, nor our molars made by millstone makers, nor our "ducts" made by plumbers.

---

2. Xenophon, *Memorabilia*, trans. E. C. Marchant, Loeb Classical Library 168 (Cambridge, MA: Harvard University Press, 2013), 57.

Yes, those are differences between the items (human arti-facts on one hand and the human body on the other), but not *relevant* differences. Socrates's argument goes from human forethought to divine forethought, not from human forethought to human forethought.

The art of finding relevant differences, of making help-ful distinctions, is a subtle one. Sometimes it requires the evolution of whole bodies of knowledge in order to grasp the deep differences between things. Sometimes it requires whole fields of science, such as evolutionary science, which allows us to specify in extreme detail exactly how different the origin of a door is from the origin of an eyelid.

Arguments about Cause

A causes B. Simple enough. Sunlight causes roses to grow. Pushing a person over a cliff causes them to plummet, pos-sibly to their death. What could be simpler than that?

Speaking of homicide, did you know that the amount of ice cream we eat increases at the same rate in our society as the amount of people who are killed? Basically, when consumption of ice cream goes up, so do cases of homicide. It gives new meaning to the cliché "we all scream for ice cream." In arguments where A causes B, our reasoning about this cold fact can be short and sweet: ice cream con-sumption causes murder (probably consumption of rum raisin ice cream in particular). Case closed. Truly, ice cream is a guilty pleasure.

Of course, a competent homicide detective would know better. One of our favorite television detectives is Detec-tive Inspector Jimmy Perez, on the BBC One series *Shet-land*. Detective Perez would ask follow-up questions, probe alternative possibilities, and, in the end, prove ice cream's innocence. But how? Stay tuned.

CORRELATION

Detective Perez is ready to investigate. First, he mulls over the main fact: when consumption of ice cream goes up, so do cases of homicide. "Freeze frame," he says, preventing us from jumping to conclusions again. *Might it be equally true to say that when cases of homicide go up, consumption of ice cream goes up?* The main fact, as stated, doesn't really clarify the direction of events. Detective Perez suspects that what causes what in this case may be the very opposite: an increase in homicide cases could cause an uptick in ice cream consumption. Sometimes people eat sweets, especially ice cream, to cope with horrible events; maybe the families of victims are grieving with a scoop or two of raspberry ripple. Might the direction of cause go the other way?

Then it hits him. "It's correlation," whispers Perez, a sparkle of insight in his eyes. But the sparkle quickly dies and his eyes darken. "This goes straight to the top: to probabilities."

What Perez has realized is that the two events, the increase of ice cream consumption and increase of homicides, are connected, but not necessarily to each other in a direct causal way. The connection may go deeper. Something—or someone!—may be behind *both* events. Perez has hit upon a deep principle in critical thinking: *correlation does not necessarily imply causation.*

Consider Zach and Samira, perfect strangers. Zach is from Vermont. Samira is from Lebanon. They're both visiting Boston, Massachusetts, on a Monday and happen to cross paths at a cross street. Strangely enough, both are wearing the same shade of blue: Zach's shirt is periwinkle blue and Samira's scarf is periwinkle blue. Coordinated periwinkles, yes, but are these *correlated* periwinkles? In this case, no. This is just a one-off coincidence. One circumstance did not cause the other, nor did a third thing (e.g., "Celebrate Periwinkle Day" in Boston—not a real holiday, alas) cause both periwinkles to co-occur.

But now consider that Zach and Samira cross paths the next day in Boston and, once more, both are wearing periwinkle blue. Zach wears a periwinkle scarf and Samira wears a periwinkle shirt. Then the next day, at the same cross street, they cross paths again in their periwinkle items. Now both are wearing periwinkle shirts. By Thursday, Zach and Samira are both wearing a periwinkle scarf and a periwinkle shirt, and meeting at the same cross street, but this time, they both enter a Vietnamese café for lunch together. What was at first a coincidence seems to have become a correlation: Zach and Samira noticed a random periwinkle partner and, testing the waters by wearing periwinkle the next day at the same cross street, found a kindred soul in the other. One thing led to another and then to a first date.

Detective Perez, naturally, knows the story of how Zach and Samira met and fell in love. He knows how correlation and causation can play games with the mind. In the case of the "ice cream homicides," he knows that increased ice cream consumption and increased homicides are more similar to Zach and Samira's "periwinkle situation" on Thursday than their periwinkle situation on that first day, Monday. Ice cream consumption and homicide rates are not a one-off coincidence; this is a repeating pattern. This is lunch at the Vietnamese café.

CAUSATION

So, there may be a *common cause* between these two events that is pulling all the strings, but how could we say that for sure? If there is indeed a third thing, a lurking variable, that explains this correlation, how could we know?

Now here is why they pay Detective Perez the big bucks, or, rather, the big British pounds. Perez knows that he needs a candidate for "common cause." So, he brings in some suspects. One after another, the suspects are cleared. Alibis are corroborated. Plot twists are provided. No luck. Finally, near the end of the episode, he narrows it down to one suspect: high temperature. Perez concludes that high temperatures are the common cause between the increase in ice cream consumption and homicides. When temperatures rise, people like to gobble down a cooling scoop of ice cream. Similarly, when temperatures rise, people also hit the bars or beaches and get brawly, so they might be more likely to kill others. Yet, Perez needs proof of his hypothesis.

Let's follow his process. First, he takes the facts at hand and uses a shorthand to refer to them:

IC = Ice cream consumption increases
H = Homicide rate increases
T = Temperature increases

Perez knows that the probability of H when IC is true is *higher* than the probability of H alone. In formal notation, this looks like:

$Pr(H|IC) > Pr(H)$

This can be read as "the probability of H *given* IC is greater than the probability of H." Let's translate that a bit. Imagine you ask Perez the question "What is the homicide rate right now?" Without further information available to him, Perez would offer the usual homicide statistics. Let's just say that the usual homicide rate is around 1 percent of the population (our imaginary percentage is unrealistically high, thankfully). Perez would answer, "Around 1 percent of the population." However, if you then told Perez that ice cream consumption is up, it would change his answer; he would know the homicide rate is probably now higher than the baseline 1 percent.

This works the other way around as well:

$$Pr(IC|H) > Pr(IC)$$

"What is the rate of ice cream consumption?" Without further information, it is the usual baseline rate. With the further information of an increased homicide rate, we know it is likely *above* the usual baseline rate.

Yet so far, we've only repeated the fact that increased rates of ice cream consumption and homicide are correlated. We already knew that. Perez now introduces his suspected common cause: temperature increases (T). We'll need two formulas:

1. $Pr(H|IC \text{ and } T) = Pr(H|T)$
2. $Pr(H|IC \text{ and not-}T) = Pr(H|\text{not-}T)$

First, let's translate both formulas into less abstract forms:

1. The probability of H given IC *and* T is equal to the probability of H given T.
2. The probability of H given IC *and* not-T is equal to the probability of H given not-T.

This is a simple idea, despite the dry formal language (which is helpful in boiling down otherwise long-winded sentences). Don't worry if you don't follow any of this on the first reading. Sometimes it takes a second reading, or a third, for something subtle like this to really click. Read the following slowly and carefully, and read it twice, at minimum. Case 1 says that when temperatures are up, the fact that ice cream consumption is up does not make an increase in homicides any likelier. Case 2 says that when temperatures are *not* up, the fact that ice cream consumption is up does not make an increase in homicides any likelier. In other words, ice consumption has no real effect on homicide rates once one accounts for temperature increases. You can see this in the formulas: IC adds no value to the probability of H. It simply melts away.

So, Detective Perez has screened off the correlation and nabbed his suspect: the heat! In Shetland, which is cold and wet most of the year, understandable given its location in the far north, it is perhaps no surprise that heat would cause such a disturbance—a disturbance so sweet, and yet so fatal.

THE HARD PART OF ARGUMENTS ABOUT CAUSE

Now, the hard part of arguments about cause is differentiating correlations from causation in the real world, which is rarely a simple endeavor. Detective Perez makes it look easy, but unfortunately, he is a fictional person. In our chaotic and mostly nonfictional world, finding the real causes of things is hard. Some philosophers, such as David Hume, are not even sure that anything causes anything. For Hume, it is just correlation all the way down, with no causal connections. It doesn't get harder than that to make a compelling argument about cause.

That is an extreme view, however. The task of the thinker is to do their due diligence in screening off spurious correlations and getting nearer to the heart of how A causes B, or whether or not A actually causes B. This task can be done with exquisite precision, as in the sciences, or more intuitively, as in an intro level essay for a college course.

LOGICAL PITFALLS

Gaps in Reasoning

"To err is human," writes the eighteenth-century English poet Alexander Pope in his lengthy poem *An Essay on Criticism*. Our cognitive powers, understandably, are not divine. Everyone, at some point, has fumbled in their reasoning. Whether it is overgeneralization (as in the previous sentence) or appeal to a majority (as in the next sentence), we're error-prone mammals. It's true, since most people agree with us on that.

Admitting that we have a problem is the first step in recovery. Seeking help is the next step. Not everyone gets to step 1, and of those who do, many don't continue on to step 2. Step 3 is rethinking reasoning, reimagining its role in our lives, and reemphasizing how delicate, intricate, and artlike it is. Reasoning is not an easy art, nor a finished one. It evolves in this way and that, and will ever continue to do so. As Scott L. Pratt, professor of philosophy at the University of Oregon, told us,

> Reasoning as it has developed in the West, and as it is presently taught and learned, is meant to ensure a world where there are no contradictions, no ambiguous middle grounds, and stability in identity, so that classes and categories (especially those of advantage and power) remain in place. Resistance to oppression by critical reasoning is bound to replicate the same kinds of categories it challenges. Real resistance requires looking for different ways of engaging and thinking about the world—as in some Indigenous thought, for example—that seek value and purpose not constrained by the structures of Western reasoning.

Professor Pratt's point is vital. There exist many different ways of engaging and thinking about the world, including many prematurely dismissed as peripheral, primitive, or simply mistaken. One might consider, for example, the revival of logical traditions from Buddhist thinkers such as Nagarjuna (c. 150–c.250 CE) and the Tibetan philosopher Gorampa (1429–89 CE).

Having studied and taught the historical development of philosophy, we've come to believe that the two abiding virtues of a good reasoner are charity and clarity. Charity involves interpreting an argument fairly and carefully, even to the point of supplementing the argument with reasonable clarifications and amendments. Clarity involves a desire to create relations of mutual understanding between oneself and others. Both charity and clarity are social virtues, not merely intellectual virtues. Both virtues require a decent degree of respect for other persons. The most common gap in reasoning, to be frank, is the sheer disregard for the reasoning of others, which often arises from a disregard for others. Without charity and clarity, there is little to no reasoning possible. Sometimes the gap in our reasoning is in the shape of another person—sometimes a stranger speaking an unfamiliar language, or using an unfamiliar logic.

Fallacies

Perhaps you have been accused of "committing a fallacy," and felt ashamed for it, as if you had committed a sin or crime. We feel the shame of this scarlet "F" when it is applied to our views, especially those core views that make up the heart of who we are. For philosophers, it is the more awful F-word. But, as Jesus allegedly said, "Let him who is without sin among you be the first to throw a stone at her."[3]

---

3. John 8:7, English Standard Version.

Jesus wasn't condoning sin, but merely telling the wolfish mob to check their own hypocrisy and, in a genuine come-to-Jesus moment, forgive the sins of others. Fallacies are arguably *not* moral violations, so let us be even more forgiving. Yes, fallacies and critical thinking are not friends, so it is essential that we identify and avoid fallacies when we put on our critical thinking caps, but don't become one of those people who throws around "That's a fallacy!" like that old mob throwing stones.

What is a fallacy? *Fallacy* is the fancy term for a slip-up in reasoning. Fallacies come in countless flavors, since slip-ups in reasoning come in countless flavors. Some flavors are well known, like *argumentum ad hominem*. Some are obscure, like the "fallacy of misplaced concreteness."

The term "fallacy" comes from the Latin *fallacia*, which means a deceit or trick, from the Latin *fallere*, "to deceive." Now, if we told you that this etymology shows us the true or only correct meaning of the term "fallacy," we would be committing the etymological fallacy, which is the error of claiming that the history of a term, oftentimes the *ancient* history of a term, is the true or only correct meaning of that term. The word "nice" derives from the Latin *nescius*, which means "unknowing," "ignorant," or "unaware." Therefore, when you call your professors nice, as you so often do, you *must* mean that your professors are ignorant. Does that sound right to you? Hopefully not.

Fallacies are slippery fish. They slip in and out of arguments, often without anyone noticing. They swim unnoticed in plain sight, since they're so often similar in appearance to good reasoning. It takes some training to catch them. We can start that training with a simple taxonomic division of fallacies into "formal" or "informal." A formal fallacy is an error related specifically to the validity of the argument (recall validity from the previous section). Informal fallacies are all the other slip-ups in reasoning (it's a big list). An example of each may help make the distinction more concrete for you.

AN EXAMPLE OF A FORMAL FALLACY

Either the sun is hot or Pluto is cold. The sun is hot. Therefore, Pluto is not cold.

The formal structure of this fallacy is as follows: P or Q. P. Therefore, not Q. This fallacy is called "Affirming a Disjunct." Why is this a problem? Recall our discussion of validity and invalidity, in which we specified that a deductively valid argument is an argument in which, if the premises are true, the conclusion cannot be false. Well, let's consider our example closely.

P1. Either the sun is hot or Pluto is cold.
P2. The sun is hot
C. Therefore, Pluto is not cold.

"The sun is hot" is true, so P2 is true. P1 is true as well, but in a less clear way. "Either the sun is hot or Pluto is cold" can be true in three ways: (1) The sun is hot; (2) Pluto is cold; or (3) The sun is hot and Pluto is cold. P1 is called a disjunction. A disjunction is true if at least one of its "disjuncts" (the statements connected by "or") are true. Since both disjuncts of P1 are true, P1 is most definitely true. Finally, C is clearly false, since Pluto is indeed cold. So, this argument gives true premises *and* a false conclusion; thus, it is invalid. All formal fallacies are invalid arguments, but each makes a unique mistake, and for that, we think they deserve special names, such as "Affirming a Disjunct."

AN EXAMPLE OF AN INFORMAL FALLACY

If chocolate scones are delicious, then the quantum particles that constitute chocolate scones must be delicious.

Chocolate scones are delicious. Therefore, the quantum particles that constitute chocolate scones must be delicious.

Believe it or not, this is a valid argument, a *modus ponens* argument to be precise: If P, then Q. P. Therefore Q. Yet this valid argument is fallacious. The fallacy it commits is the fallacy of division, in which some property of a whole thing is erroneously attributed to the parts of that whole. A chocolate scone may be delicious, but the quantum particles that constitute chocolate scones are not delicious. A dog is man's best friend, but the liver of a dog is not man's best friend.

Avoiding Common Fallacies

Our species seems to love fault-finding: witness the books and websites abounding with long inventories of fallacies. We highly recommend browsing these, especially if you wish to decode your social media feed. One of the best online fallacy lists is Wikipedia's "List of Fallacies," from which we've chosen six examples we consider ubiquitous and deleterious to public discourse. *Consider them the worst of the worst.* As we cover these fallacies, we intend to zoom out from each example into a more general discussion of reasoning. We will contrast poor reasoning with better reasoning and, most importantly, try to impress on you just how personal, how frustrating, even how destructive failures of reasoning can be. If you've ever suffered from the poor reasoning of others, or if you've ever flung a rotten argument at others and felt guilty after the fact, you'll want to read this subsection carefully.

Let's begin with a metafallacy, a fallacy that warns us against misuse of our ability to find fallacies.

THE FALLACY FALLACY

> *My cousin said that "$2+2=4$," and my cousin is mighty smart, so it's true that "$2+2=4$."*

This argument is fallacious, yes, but that doesn't mean that the claim "$2+2=4$" is false. If we were to conclude that "$2+2=4$" is false *because* of this fallacious reasoning, then we are committing the fallacy fallacy. You can attach a shoddy argument to any claim, but you don't thereby falsify that claim. Did we falsify "$2+2=4$" by basing its truth on the testimony and intelligence of our cousin? No.

The fallacy fallacy may be the Internet's favorite fallacy, if frequency of use is any indication of preference. Many people often want victory in argument, not truth. They aim for refutation above all else. They may think that if you use a fallacy in defense of claim A, then claim A is refuted. *Your argument is fallacious, so your political claim is absurd.* This is poor reasoning.

STRAW MAN FALLACY

The straw man fallacy is perhaps the Internet's second-favorite fallacy. It looks something like this:

John: Some people think that a minimum wage improves the quality of life for workers.

Carl: So, you're saying that we should simply listen to this anonymous group of "some people," who provide no evidence, but only "think" that a minimum wage helps some small fraction of workers to buy a little more avocado toast on the weekend? That's insane!

Carl is a jerk. But apart from that, what has gone wrong here, in terms of his reasoning? Carl distorted John's claim. Carl presented a caricature, aka a "Straw Man," of John's modest claim, and then Carl rejected that caricature. Like

Dr. Frankenstein, Carl created his own monster and then rejected it. Did Carl refute John's actual claim? No, but he will say he did, because, again, Carl is a jerk.

Straw-manning should be contrasted with, and remedied by, its opposite force: *steel-manning*. Steel-manning is another name for applying the principle of charity, which means interpreting an argument fairly and carefully, even to the point of supplementing the argument with reasonable clarifications and amendments. You strengthen an argument with steel, rather than stuff it with straw. Let's listen to Kathleen steel-man John's argument:

Kathleen: Some people, I imagine you mean economists, think that a minimum wage helps workers meet their basic needs, such as food and housing. Do I understand you correctly?

Kathleen not only interprets John's argument charitably, with a steel-man version, but she also asks if her interpretation is correct. That is reasoning done beautifully.

FALSE ALTERNATIVES

You are either part of the problem or part of the solution.

That's a bit of a scary thought, isn't it? If you're not helping someone, you're hurting them. Such alternatives often push you into an uncomfortable corner and force you to pick your position on the left wall or right wall. The fallacy of false alternatives, sometimes called the false dilemma fallacy (although there can be more than just two false options), is a way to mislead us into prematurely narrowing our philosophical options.

Often, false alternatives are unequal: one option is better than the other. This is usually no accident. Many people want others to agree with them on any number of issues, so they sometimes try to force a choice between their view and some weaker view. In our example above, which option sounds better (generally speaking): being part of a problem or being part of a solution?

You can resist false alternatives by suggesting an *alternative* that wasn't provided, or by taking both alternatives as simultaneously true. Red pill or blue pill? What about the green pill? Or what about taking both the red and blue pill? Some alternatives may seem both mutually exclusive (meaning that if one is true, the other cannot be true) *and* exhaustive of all possibilities. But always look closer. For example, it may seem that either determinism or free will is the case; it can't be both, and one *must* be the case. But then comes the philosophical position known as compatibilism. As the name suggests, compatibilism is the view that two or more things are compatible, or can be true together; in this case, the compatibilist holds that free will and determinism are both true. We will let you look up the details of this subtle view, but be assured that compatibilism is a serious metaphysical alternative to the usual dichotomy of free will *or* determinism. So, when confronted by a seemingly inescapable set of alternatives, always remember that some thinkers are compatibilists where no compatibility seems possible. You can use your deterministic free will to join their refined ranks and suggest a third or middle way through the fog.

Below are three examples of false alternatives. Consider ways in which you could reject each dilemma:

1. Either Karl Marx is correct about capitalist economies or Adam Smith is correct about capitalist economies.
2. Either Socrates was a bad philosopher or he wasn't a philosopher at all.
3. Moral truths cannot be grounded in natural phenomena, so they must be grounded in Biblical truth.

COMPLEX QUESTION

Does your poor mother know you're terrible at logic?

Similar to the fallacy of false alternatives, the fallacy of the complex question attempts to trap your thinking into a small set of *presupposed* false alternatives. *Are you still a terrible logician?* That question presupposes that you *were* a terrible logician. If you were never a terrible logician, then that presupposition is false and the question is a complex question.

As with false alternatives, complex questions can be overcome by breaking out of the narrow options on offer. With a complex question, step back and interrogate what the question *presupposes*. Like a sly politician, don't immediately accept all questions as good questions. Take questions apart. Test them. In two words: question questions. If they presuppose falsehoods, call out those falsehoods and reject the question.

ARGUMENTUM AD HOMINEM

The *argumentum ad hominem* ("argument against the person") is well known, yet still widely used. Whenever a claim is said to be refuted on account of some feature of the person who made the claim, you've likely got yourself an *ad hominem*.

> *Carl claims that morality is universal and objective, but Carl is a jerk, so that's nonsense.*

This clear-cut case of an *ad hominem* argument shows why this line of reasoning is fallacious, but let's replace Carl's metaethical claim to get a clearer sense of why.

> *Carl claims that "$2 + 2 = 4$," but Carl is a jerk, so that's nonsense.*

Did we just refute "$2+2=4$"? No. In a similar way, we did not refute the claim that morality is universal and objective. We merely insulted Carl—and ourselves, with bad reasoning. Of course, there are possible substitutions that would help this argument:

> *Carl claims that Carl is not a jerk, but Carl is a jerk, so that's nonsense.*

In this case, claiming that Carl is a jerk is relevant to refuting the claim that Carl is *not* a jerk. This is different from claiming that Carl is a jerk, when Carl's jerkiness has no relevance to the claim in question. Relevance is key. If some feature of the person is *relevant* to the argument, then it is not an *ad hominem* fallacy to involve that feature in the argument.

Carl: I am an expert in logic.
Kathleen: Based on my careful research into your history, including your education, there is no evidence that you are an expert in logic.
Carl: *Ad hominem! Ad hominem! Ad hominem!* Attacking the person!

Because the claim that Carl is an expert in logic is relevant, this is not an *ad hominem* fallacy.

ARGUMENTUM AD HOMINEM TU QUOQUE

An extension of the *argumentum ad hominem* is the *argumentum ad hominem tu quoque*. *Tu quoque* means "you also." This is basically an appeal to hypocrisy.

John: You should eat healthier foods, Carl.
Carl: You never eat healthy food! What a load of codswallop! Oh yessiree, I saw those triple chocolate scones in your sock drawer!

Carl has changed the subject to John's hypocrisy as a way of rejecting the claim. Yet the claim may remain true; it may be that Carl should eat healthier food due to his quickly deteriorating health, whereas John, who has been and remains in peak physical condition, is not subject to any pressing need to eat healthy foods. But Carl is defensive and needs a dirty trick to feel safe again. Poor Carl.

A common form of the *tu quoque* fallacy occurs in politics, where it is known as "whataboutism." Your preferred political party has been accused of a misdeed, so, in a fit of defensive irrationality, you effectively reject the accusation by accusing the other party of the same or a similar misdeed. Case closed, you think. Two wrongs have magically made a right. Unfortunately not.

It is a bitter truth, but hypocrites can be right. Pointing to their hypocrisy does not refute their claim. It feels like it should, but it doesn't. If a hypocrite claims that you committed a moral offense, their having committed the same offense does not mean that you did not commit that offense, too. Truth can come from anywhere, even from utter hypocrites, even from poor Carl. Let's never deny the truth, even if it comes from the mouths of jerks, knuckleheads, creeps, gadflies, and arrogant dizzy-eyed barnacles.

MOTIVATING AN ARGUMENT: GETTING YOUR AUDIENCE TO CARE

Let's say you avoid these logical pitfalls and craft an argument that you think is a strong one. Well done. "You still need to sell it," explained UMKC philosophy professor Clancy Martin in a recent conversation about logic and argumentation. You still have to *motivate* your reader. Motivating arguments get an audience to care: to care about the intellectual context in which the argument is situated, or to care about the implications and stakes of your conclusion, or to care enough to read your words to the very end. How do you construct such a motivating argument? You need to explain why your conclusion and its attendant premises should matter to your intended readers. The argument does not necessarily have to matter to your reader as it matters to you (your interest might be rather personal and particularly idiosyncratic), but it needs to matter nonetheless.

Remember that writing, at its best, is the act of showing a reader something they have never seen before, but desperately *need* to. An argument's motivation should always appeal to a reader's needs, desires, fears, interests, and proclivities. This is not the same as pandering to a reader. The most important arguments are often as disturbing as they are compelling, but they always encourage their audience to persist despite the discomfort for a number of important reasons. Let's quickly run through a range of tactics for motivating an argument and offer a number of *signal phrases* that alert a reader to the significance of the thesis.

Tactics of Motivation

OVERTURNING COMMON KNOWLEDGE

Aristotle once said that all critical thinking begins in recognizing the commonly held positions on a given topic, what he called the *endoxa*.[4] Critical thinking is never satisfied by the *endoxa* for very long, and attempts to question common knowledge, the assumptions and beliefs we often unreflectively hold dear. An argument's power, its ability to motivate a reader's attention, often depends on its overturning some long-held or engrained way of thinking. For example, most people think that following the "Law of the Land" is morally required. Martin Luther King Jr., in his

---

4. Aristotle, *Introductory Readings*, trans. Terence Irwin and Gail Fine (Indianapolis: Hackett, 1996), 331.

"Letter from Birmingham Jail," argued that one has a moral obligation to *break* laws that are unjust, citing the Christian philosopher St. Augustine in defense of such civil disobedience: "I would agree with St. Augustine that 'An unjust law is no law at all.'"[5]

> *Signal Phrase*: "*While many assume* that drone warfare is a more accurate and therefore a more humane form of combat, I will demonstrate that it poses a moral danger precisely because of this assumption."

REVEALING AN INCONSISTENCY

There are many famous theories that depend on interlocking arguments. Unearthing a weakness in a particular theory or set of arguments is a nice way to break scholarly ground for yourself, but also interest readers in the scholarly debate. Similarly, challenging a well-established paradigm by proposing an alternative explanation for the facts is motivating, at the very least, for those committed to the old picture of reality.

> *Signal Phrase*: "America's Founding Fathers suggested that their new nation should be based on life, liberty, and the pursuit of happiness, *yet in many cases they* acted in such a way to *undermine* these universal ideals, most pointedly by their relationship to the slave trade."

THERE IS A PUZZLE

Some theses reveal, rather than solve, an intellectual puzzle. When Richard Gale, a contemporary American philosopher, wrote *The Divided Self of William James*, he

---

5. Martin Luther King Jr., "Letter from Birmingham Jail," in *Why We Can't Wait* (New York: Signet Books, 1964), 82.

claimed that there were two largely antithetical lines of thinking in the writing of the founder of American pragmatism, William James. There was the "Promethean James," who believed the meaning of life consisted in acting freely, and the "Mystical Poo-Baa James," who held that human meaning was a matter of getting in touch with, and being receptive to, something like God. Gale's thesis outlined a puzzle: how could James hold both positions, given that they seemed so radically different? Life is often complex and contradictory. Sometimes it is sufficient for a writer to show readers how perplexing it is.

> *Signal Phrase*: "This interpretation of the causes of the Civil War, which considers a number of disparate factors, *complicates the straightforward, and inaccurate*, view that it can be traced to the issue of slavery alone."

RESOLVING A DEBATE IN THE EXISTING LITERATURE

A number of writers, maybe quite a large number, are already involved in the critical debate you are entering. They want to know what you think, especially if you think you can resolve some long-standing quarrel between well-established authors. In the scholarly literature on the Cold War, for example, there is disagreement about when this twentieth-century confrontation between the United States and the Soviet Union actually began. Some historians argue that it began immediately after World War II, others that it did not actually arise until the Korean War. Maybe you find a pivotal letter from the archives that puts the argument to rest. You will want to set your argument in the context of the aforementioned debate, and everyone in the debate will pay attention.

> *Signal Phrase*: "*I seek to resolve the long-standing disagreement* between Mark Scott and Candice Malcom

(2002 and 2006) regarding the importance of mirror neurons in feelings of compassion."

SURPRISE!

Everyone likes a good surprise when it comes to arguments. If you can promise your reader something unexpected in your conclusion, you will probably motivate them to carry through to the end. Obviously, surprises come in many forms, but writers should be on the lookout for seemingly insignificant aspects of a topic and then look at them very carefully to see if they are actually insignificant. Sometimes they are not, and a beautiful, motivating argument can be made.

> *Signal Phrase*: "*New data reveals a dramatic trend* in the rate of death among bread-eating individuals."

DIAMOND IN THE ROUGH

Similar to "motivation by surprise," finding an undiscovered diamond in the literature is always a good way to seize and hold a reader's attention. Diamonds can be poems, papers, passages, and the like that are often ignored by scholars, the secret etymological origins of words from a text, or comparisons between authors that have hitherto remained undiscussed. Think like Ezra Pound, and "Make it new!"

> *Signal Phrase*: "*Recent archival discoveries shed new light* on the relationship between Martin Luther King Jr. and his perspective on modern feminism."

EXTRAPOLATION

Making an argument in a narrow context can have much broader implications on the thinking of a reader. Motivating arguments often encourage readers to extrapolate from a single case to similar like instances. Extrapolation is the act of estimating or concluding something by assuming that existing trends will continue or a current method will remain applicable. If you make an argument about the destruction of a particular wetland or bog in your neighborhood, readers might be able to extrapolate from your findings, and come to a much larger conclusion about environmental degradation in the Northeast United States or, more significantly, the world at large. Ideally, you want to signal or point them in the direction of this extrapolation.

> *Signal Phrase*: "This study, which highlights the instability of the Icon's front axle, *stands to be the first of* many which will transform the auto industry."

Once you realize the motivation of your argument, you will notice how it is inextricably tied to the argument's structure, to the logical steps that you will outline for a reader. We will spend the next chapter thinking through the nuts and bolts of argumentative structure.

EXERCISES

1. We began this chapter with the question "what is an argument?" To answer that question, we explored the nature of premises, inferences, validity, and soundness. Using what you learned, make up one deductively valid, but unsound argument, and then make up one sound argument. We'll help you get started by giving our own examples.

   (i) Example of a deductively valid, but unsound argument:

   Premise 1: All textbooks are error-free.
   Conclusion: Some textbooks are error-free.

Remember, a deductively valid argument is an argument in which, if the premises are true, the conclusion cannot be false. If it is true that "all textbooks are error-free," then our conclusion cannot be false, since it simply asserts that "some" textbooks are error-free, which must be true if "all" textbooks are error-free. If all cats are mammals, then necessarily some cats are mammals. Put differently, it cannot be false that some cats are mammals and simultaneously true that all cats are mammals. Therefore, our above argument is deductively valid.

As for soundness, remember that a sound argument is an argument that is deductively valid and whose premises are actually true. Our above example argument is deductively valid, but is it sound? Do you think it is true that all textbooks are error-free? Neither do we.

(ii) Example of a sound argument:

Premise 1: $1+1=2$.
Conclusion: $1+1=2$.

Here we have a deductively valid argument (how could it be true that "one plus one equals two" and simultaneously false that "one plus one equals two"?). We also have a sound argument here, since it is actually true that "one plus one equals two."

This example shows you that sound arguments aren't always interesting or helpful, but can be repetitive, trivial, and dull. Sound arguments are necessary for good thinking and writing, but not sufficient.

2. Take a look back at our "Avoiding Common Fallacies" section. Sometimes, to help one avoid fallacies, it

helps to intentionally make those fallacies, to better acquaint oneself with what one is so carefully avoiding. So let's acquaint ourselves in this way. Create an argument for each of the informal fallacies that we covered above, from the "fallacy fallacy" to the *argumentum ad hominem tu quoque*. In other words, concoct six fallacious arguments!

(i) Example of an argument that uses the fallacy of "False Alternatives":

Premise 1: The only way to avoid a terrorist attack is to wage a preemptive war against our enemies.

Premise 2: All rational people want to avoid a terrorist attack.

Conclusion: Therefore, all rational people will support a preemptive war against our enemies.

Analysis: Our example argument shows how subtle a "false alternative" fallacy can be. There is no clear "either-or" language in this argument, and yet there is a presumption that there are only two options: (1) don't wage a preemptive war and therefore get attacked; or (2) wage preemptive war and therefore avoid attack. What makes this a "false" alternative is the fact that there can be other ways to avoid such attacks that do not involve preemptive war. All told, be vigilant out there, because false alternatives are prevalent!

3. The earth cannot be round *because* [. . .]. First, fill in the bracket with an irrelevant or obviously absurd "reason," the more bizarre the better, and then give your new fallacy a fun name. For example: The earth

cannot be round because [if it were round, then there wouldn't be flat-earthers]. This is the fallacy of "Someone believes it, so it can't be wrong." Let's call it, in bad Latin, *argumentum ad credentis* (argument to the believer). Try to invent two fallacies.

Chapter 3

THINKING THROUGH STRUCTURE

ARGUMENTATIVE STRUCTURE

Most essays—in both academic settings and popular media—lead a reader through a series of ideas in order to propose a particular conclusion. A conclusion is that one provoking thought that you as the writer are trying to communicate to the reader in the course of your writing. To build toward a conclusion, you need to carefully craft a strong structure to your writing. Think about essay structure as the particular steps you take (that you must take) in the course of an essay to guide a reader's understanding.

When you write an essay, what you are aiming to do is map out the logical moves a reader must follow in order to reach your conclusion. You probably know that a paper needs a beginning (an introduction), a middle (the body), and an end (a conclusion). But what goes in the middle, and what order those middle parts go in, is not so easy. Their placement—in the "body" of your essay, between the introduction and conclusion—depends on you. And this is why it is necessary to think about argumentative structure.

Reading is chronological (it happens from one moment to the next), linear (from this word to the following word), and sequential (every word is ordered for the sake of the whole making sense). Structuring your writing is about putting the right words in the right order, one at a time. We are reminded of Stephen King's comment about the stepwise process of writing: "When asked, 'How do you write?' I invariably answer, 'One word at a time,' and the answer is invariably dismissed. But that is all it is. It sounds too simple to be true, but consider the Great Wall of China, if you will: one stone at a time, man. That's all. One stone at a time. But I've read you can see that motherfucker from space without a telescope."[1] And what a reader should see, in your essay, is a well-ordered construction: if not a monumental wall, at least a well-marked path to follow along your thinking.

Classical Structure

Arguments have a long history, tracing back more than 2,500 years, and they have taken a variety of forms. Ancient Greek and Roman politicians and rhetoricians typically followed what is now regarded as the classical structure. You don't need to remember the Latin names for the various moments of an argument, but you will recognize the logic of the steps. That is the important part.

1. Introduce your argument by winning the goodwill and interest of an audience while setting out the topic to be discussed. (*Exordium*)
2. Give the relevant facts of the case, the "when," "where," "who," and "what" of the issue. (*Narratio*)
3. Make any distinctions necessary to understand the topic, and explain what your claim is and what it is not. (*Partitio*)
4. Provide good support for your claim. Don't forget that this can be factual or logical in nature. (*Confirmatio*)
5. Consider and express the counterarguments and the evidence used to justify the opposing view or views. (*Refutatio*)

---

1. Stephen King, "A Preface in Two Parts," in *The Stand* (New York: Anchor Books, 2012), x.

6. Summarize the findings of the case and close the argument. (*Peroratio*)

We are not suggesting that this argumentative structure will fit your needs in every case, but it does express what is roughly needed in an effective argumentative essay. Basically, you need to say something like the following: "Kind gentlepeople, let me interest you in my topic. These are the facts of the matter. Given these facts, this is the claim I would like you to consider. I think you might notice that I am talking about this part of the topic and not other parts. Let me provide reasons for my claim. Some think there are better claims to explain the facts of the matter. Interesting. I don't, but let me explain why. I will now close the case by restating my claim. Game, set, match, *me*."

Structure Redux

The order of the parts of an argumentative essay will be determined by the sort of argument you want to present in your paper. That is another way of saying that the structure of your paper depends on your thesis and the methods for providing support to your thesis that you laid out in your introduction. What you are doing when you map the structure of an essay is basically saying to yourself: "What does my reader need to know first, *then* what does she need to know, what evidence does she *then* need to see, and what does she *then* need to acknowledge *at last* to be convinced thoroughly?"

Thinking through your structure is about figuring out the "thens" of your paper, or the "what comes nexts," in order to deliver your conclusion. Many professors suggest that students create an outline before writing an essay, and this is not a bad idea, but it tends to skip over an important step in the process. A writer, first, needs to complete a simple exercise that begins to do the work of a good outline; we call it the "structure redux paragraph." This is a template for a paragraph that we have students write before they create an outline. The paragraph should go something like this:

> Dear reader, let me explain what I am going to do in the course of this essay. The question I am going to ask is QQQQQQQ. The answer to this question, and the claim I will make in this essay is YYYYYYY. For you, dear reader, to accept my claim you first need to (VERB) AAAAAAAA. The next thing that you must (VERB) is BBBBBBBBBBB. The next thing that you must (VERB) is CCCCCCCCC. The reader may want to consider XXXXXXXXX counterarguments for a different view. Finally, my hope is the reader will agree with ZZZZZZZZZZ.

Note well: This paragraph should not find its way into your actual essay. It is a prewriting exercise. In the exercise, you will notice that you need to pick the "verb" in several cases and fill in the question, conclusion, and premises. The "verb" will be things like how your reader needs to "see" or "acknowledge" a certain aspect of the topic or argument. In other cases, a reader may need to "understand" something about the topic or argument, or "evaluate" a comparison (whether similar or different) that you establish in your argument. And then there will be times when a reader must "accept" or "be convinced by" a proposition or set of premises you offer. You are responsible for filling in the blanks of the "structure paragraph redux," and it will be different for every author, and for every essay.

Ordering Premises

Here's an interesting truth about formal arguments: the order of the premises frequently does not matter. (What order you count your three apples, five strawberries, and two bananas doesn't make a difference to the conclusion that you have ten fruits.) But in the art of writing, the ordering of premises in an argument almost always does matter a great deal. Think about an article in zoology that talks about the anatomy of mammals. It has a few simple premises, set out in the following order. This is a poorly ordered argument:

1. Rabbits are mammals.
2. Humans are mammals.
3. Cows are mammals.
4. All mammals are warm-blooded.

   Therefore, rabbits, humans, and cows are warm-blooded.

There is nothing formally incorrect about this argument, but it would not read very well in the current ordering of premises. Why? Think about working through the essay and coming across premises 1–3. They are repetitive, yet uninteresting. There is no way that a reader could anticipate the conclusion by reading 1–3. Arriving at premise 4, a reader has to "pick up," or retrieve from memory, 1–3 in order to reach the conclusion. Now consider this order:

1. All mammals are warm-blooded.
2. Cows are mammals.
3. Humans are mammals.
4. Rabbits are mammals.

   Therefore, rabbits, humans, and cows are warm-blooded.

We think this is a much more interesting order of the same premises. If a reader finds these premises ordered like this in a long paragraph, they will be better positioned to follow along toward the conclusion. Using the initial premise ("All mammals are warm-blooded") as a key organizing claim, readers can more clearly see how the subsequent premises fit into the logical structure of the conclusion. This is all to say that the ordering of your premises determines, in large part, the ease and intrigue with which a reader will arrive at your conclusion. In the last chapter, we suggested that it is a useful practice to identify the premises in writings that you are assigned or read in your free time. This is true, but it is equally important to evaluate the ordering of the premises, to think about the structure (or sequence) of an author's argument.

If you are having trouble figuring out a good order for your premises, you might want to retrace the steps that you took to arrive at the conclusion in the first place. Say you want to argue the following: "I will argue that wealthy people have a moral obligation to give money to anyone suffering from disease, famine, or natural disaster." How did you reach this conclusion? Maybe you heard about a famine in some remote corner of the globe and went on-line to read news articles about how the famine is causing deaths and suffering to innocent children. Then, maybe you thought that innocent deaths and suffering are really bad. And then you thought that if you have the power to stop something bad from happening, you should do it. And then you thought that if you don't try to stop the suffering, then that is morally wrong. And then you thought if it is wrong to not do anything to help stop the suffering, then you have a moral obligation to help (to some degree). And then you took out your phone and made a donation to the aid foundations involved in famine relief. Bing, bang, boom. If a certain line of reasoning (ordering of premises) worked for you, then it might be the same line of reasoning you want to communicate to the reader. Try it. Peter Singer wrote one of the most famous essays in modern ethics using this ordering of these premises in "Famine, Affluence, and Morality."[2] A well-structured essay follows a natural line of reasoning for any (or at least most) critical thinkers, and that includes you.

Providing Context

Most philosophers would like their students to believe that an argument's success depends on the supporting premises alone. For better or for worse, that is simply not the case. Readers need the context, or necessary background information, in which to understand the various claims of an argument. Context is the environment in which a topic or argument lives. Describing this environment or context might seem excessive and unnecessary to you, but that is probably because you already know the context around the argument. So, take pity on your reader and give them a clue (if they don't already have one).

Providing context is always a balancing act—as is all writing and speaking—between saying too much and not saying enough. Your use of context should establish you as a kind of expert on the topic and provide a setting in which the reader can understand the significance of your forthcoming premises. But context should not overwhelm your argument. If you are writing about the obligation to donate money to relief funds, you should mention some context about the widespread existence of famines and give a kind of picture of the associated suffering, but the stories you include to provide this context should not overwhelm or distract from the argument you are presenting. This balance between wider context and focused argument is precisely what Singer accomplishes so nicely in "Famine, Affluence, and Morality."

---

2. Peter Singer, "Famine, Affluence, and Morality," *Philosophy and Public Affairs* 1, no. 3 (Spring 1972): 229–43.

Where does context usually appear in an essay? Typically, context appears in the opening moments of the middle (the body) paragraphs, at the beginning or end of section breaks, and at other places where you transition from one premise or thought to another very different one. Since context sets the stage for premises, it usually appears *before* stating the premise, so think about the first half of any paragraph as a fertile area for planting your context. And ask yourself this helpful question: "Have I given my reader the necessary information to motivate them to agree with my claim?" If the answer is "No," then more context may need to be given.

Foreshadowing Conclusions

Every sentence and phrase of an essay needs to be written in service of your thesis. This question is the key test for all paragraphs: "How does this paragraph serve (or support) my thesis?" With that being said, there will be opportunities to foreshadow your conclusion throughout your essay, in the process of making your argument. Your thesis probably has a few different parts that have to be supported, possibly in a variety of ways. When you develop a supporting paragraph for part of your thesis/conclusion, you can and should call that out to the reader. What this alert does is indicate: "Hey, reader! I think I have given you enough information for you to believe at least part of my conclusion." You don't have to be that blunt, but you want to point to your thesis/conclusion repeatedly as you guide a reader through the essay.

OUTLINING

Mapping the structure of an essay can be one of the most challenging parts of writing it. Structuring a piece of writing, if we had to simplify it to a basic blueprint, depends on the ordering of the various parts of an essay, research paper, or piece of creative writing, but also making it clear, to yourself and then to your reader, the hierarchy of ideas as they emerge in your writing. Hierarchy of ideas? Yes, "hierarchy" simply refers to the way that smaller concepts and ideas are a part of broader and bigger ideas. Perhaps you have a section of an essay about creation stories from Native American cultures. In such a section, you might describe three narrower (or more specific) subjects of Apache, Navajo, and Algonquin tales. It is always a good idea to determine the order and hierarchy of subjects before you begin writing, and this is where outlining comes in.

An outline is a specific kind of prewriting that should serve as a gentle reminder to your future self about what the heck you are trying to do in your writing. If you are like us, you will often forget and will be grateful for the reminder and guidance. Most instructors will encourage their students to make outlines, but rarely do they explain what an outline is or how to construct one. Let us try. Before we do, please remember that an outline should never be regarded as an iron contract or promise of what you have to do in a paper. Your past self, the one who wrote the outline, is never as smart as your present self, who is currently researching and writing on the topic.

Reasons to Outline

Why outline? Outlines are like movie scripts. Without a script, a movie would be completely made up on the fly. That is chaos. Such movies do exist, but not many good ones; most of your favorites will have a written plan (or script) about what should happen before filming begins. A script does not need to be finished to get started writing or filming (though a rough, complete version is common), and making changes or new plans does not need to be avoided, but a movie without a solid script is likely to fail ninety-nine times out of a hundred. A script gives you dialogue, setting, pacing, the arc of the plot, production details, and so on. Similarly, an outline for your writing creates a clear guide or road map through your thoughts that, like a well-scripted movie, promises to entertain and inform an audience.

Outlines are also wonderful for writing without writing. What do we mean by that? Suppose you have an essay due in two weeks, but you don't have the energy to start writing *today*. You simply can't bear the pressure of putting fully formed thoughts into grammatically perfect sentences right now. You have some initial ideas for your essay, but nothing good or interesting. If you wrote the essay now, it would be a sloppy pile of undercooked mung beans. An outline is the perfect place to store your undercooked mung beans before you need to cook them up into a beautiful dish of an essay. You can write your ideas without having to actually go into detail. You can write "transition to the second argument" without having to actually write the transition (at least in your first draft of an outline; you might need more specificity in your later outline). You can even add "conclusion" without having to conclude anything (see the previous parenthetical note). Get it? Writing without writing.

An outline is for us unsure or lazy writers who need a map through a writing project. When we forget where we were going with a thought, our outline is there to remind us. We feel freer, since we know that our destination, our conclusion, is coming up after only one more river crossing. We won't wander off and trudge for ten days in a remote wilderness of unrelated gibberish. With an outline, the logic of time and space in an essay becomes clear: we won't waste time and we won't scribble a loopy path through space. We view the full pathway to our destinations in one godlike glimpse. Simply put, we are never lost on the page.

Types of Outline

Here is our outline for this section of our book:

I. Open with this very outline
II. Explain subject and sentence outlines
    A. Introduction (note "mixed" outline)
    B. Examples
III. Explain alphanumeric and decimal styles
    A. Introduction ("You likely noticed those Roman numerals.")
    B. Example of alphanumeric style with seven tiers
    C. Example of decimal style (mango sticky rice example)
        1. Disadvantages of the decimal style
           a) Sticky number sequences
           b) Word processor software
IV. Conclude subsection: Whatever works best for you!

SUBJECT AND SENTENCE OUTLINES

In writing your outline, remember these two kinds: "subject words" and "sentence." Outlines are written in one of these two ways (or a mixture of both, called a "mixed" outline). A subject outline gives a brief word or two on what will be covered, whereas a sentence outline, as you probably guessed, gives whole sentences. Below are examples of these outline styles:

Subject Outline

I. Epistocracy over democracy
    A. Defining terms
    B. Justice of epistocracy on its own terms
    C. Justice of epistocracy relative to democracy

Sentence Outline

I. Epistocracy is a better form of government than democracy.
   A. Epistocracy means "rule by those who know," while democracy means "rule by the people."
   B. Let's consider two arguments for and two arguments against the justice of epistocracy.
   C. Now, let's compare the merits and demerits of epistocracy in relation to those of democracy, to determine which, if either, is the better form of government.

Mixed Outline

I. Epistocracy over democracy
   A. Epistocracy means "rule by those who know," while democracy means "rule by the people."
   B. Let's consider two arguments for and two arguments against the justice of epistocracy.
   C. Justice of epistocracy relative to democracy

Many writers likely mix subject word and sentence outlines in a single outline, as that mirrors a lot of our thinking, too. Some thoughts come in undeveloped utterances, some in long soliloquies. The subject outline is good for painting broad strokes of your vision; the sentence outline is good for painting finer strokes of your vision.

ALPHANUMERIC VS. DECIMAL STYLES

You likely noticed those Roman numerals and capital letters in our example outlines. This is one popular style of organizing outlines. It is called "alphanumeric" since it alternates between letters (alphabet) and numbers. Below is an example of an alphanumeric outline that is seven tiers deep.

I. Roman numerals
   A. Capital letters
      1. Arabic numerals
         a) Lowercase letters with right parentheses
            (1) Arabic numerals in parentheses
               (a) Lowercase letters in parentheses
                   (i) Lowercase Roman numerals in parentheses

Another style of outline is the decimal outline, which may be easier to grasp than the alphanumeric style.

1. Mango sticky rice is the best dessert.
   1.1 Traditional mango sticky rice is vegan, which is more ethical than non-vegan desserts.
   1.2 Mango sticky rice is low in sugar, so it is healthier than most desserts.
   1.3 Mango sticky rice tastes heavenly!

2. Let's consider some objections to "Mango sticky rice is the best dessert."
   2.1 One sophistical objection: The concept "best dessert" has no relation to concrete realities.
   2.2 Main objection: Triple chocolate scones are, without a doubt, the best dessert.
      2.2.1 First support for main objection: Triple chocolate scones are *triple* the chocolate!
      2.2.2 Second support: They are culturally acceptable as a breakfast item.
         2.2.2.1 Evidence: I eat them for breakfast every day and no one stops me.

One disadvantage of the decimal style is how cluttered that sequence of numbers can get. You might even say that they are *sticky* sequences. Differentiating 2.2.2.1 from 2.2.1.2 and 2.1.2.1 can be a chore. And if you dive down a few more tiers in your outline using the decimal style, you might start to encounter nightmares like 1.2.2.1.1.2.1. Nevertheless, some writers like the decimal style. It does have a nice mathematical consistency to it.

Another disadvantage of the decimal style, however, is technological. Many digital writing programs, including Microsoft Word and Google Docs, automatically sort outlines into the alphanumeric style, not the decimal style. So, using the decimal style often requires more effort on your part; either you manually label and indent, or you tweak your word processor software's settings to make decimal style the automatic choice.

Whatever type and style of outline you use (e.g., subject outline in decimal style or mixed outline in alphanumeric style), never forget that this outline is a tool for *you*, not for others. Your outline is your thinking, all neatly organized in summary form. So use what feels most helpful for you and your thinking. That may even mean using a type of outline or style of outline other than the ones we've covered.

How to Create a Good Outline

Understanding the types of outlines goes a long way in beginning to think about how you might construct one. But let's be a little more specific about the process of creating a good outline.

After you finish your close reading and review your reading notes, after you work through some of the literature and begin to think about the structure of your essay (using the handy "structure redux paragraph"), after all of that you will notice that you have gathered a large number of ideas and concepts, and a certain amount of evidence, which all hang loosely around your central thesis. You probably have this material jotted down in a notebook. First, consolidate all of this prewriting onto a sheet of paper. Lay it in front of you on your desk. Yes, it might have to be a large sheet but it is important that you can see it all at once.

The first step of an outline is to label and categorize this information you will use in your essay. Things can go haywire in the attempt to categorize and order information. Sometimes it will be very hard to decide which piece of evidence belongs under what heading. Maybe you have collected a number of interesting quotations that don't fit at all. If that is the case, return to your thesis and see if these quotes you have selected serve and support your central claim. If they don't, they don't deserve to be in your paper. If they do, you may need another heading to fit them into, and you will need to place that heading somewhere within the order of other similarly sized headings.

Another challenge in outlining is knowing when and how to divide sections into subsections. There is a natural temptation to "overdivide" a topic and forget about the principle of subordination. This is what occurs below.

USELESS DIVISION IN OUTLINING

I. Nietzsche
  A. Is born
      2. In 1844
          a) In October
              (1) On the 15th

There is no need to subordinate the month and day of Nietzsche's birth, but there might be a very good reason to divide his early life into sections. For example:

I. Birth
II. Childhood
  A. Death of his father
  B. Upbringing under his mother
  C. Religious influences

III. School years
   A. Classical training
   B. Friendships
   C. Discovery of Schopenhauer

From Outline to Essay

As we mentioned at the beginning of this section, there is a danger that any outline you construct will get in the way of your future writing self's making new connections between topics, especially if your outline is already very detailed, and this could make you overlook or ignore novel, fascinating patterns of thought you didn't realize before. We would not recommend that you use your outline as the start of your writing draft; simply "write into" your outline as your essay. That is what many teachers suggest and what many students do. We suggest, instead, beginning with your strong introduction and noticing that it largely sets out the task of writing, including the sequence of context, premises, and conclusion. Your outline is a guide if you lose your way in writing, a map you can return to only if you feel yourself getting lost.

The authors of this handbook on thinking and writing have two different ways of constructing essays. John takes the "straight and narrow," working straight from beginning to end, developing things in a natural line, connecting the introduction to the first body paragraph, to the second, and so on. Jonathan, on the other hand, is a "jumper," bouncing from one section to another in order to keep momentum and allow his thinking to grow organically. Paul Bloom, a psychologist from University of Toronto and good friend, explained this difference as being possibly a function of age (although John objects to this interpretation). Bloom wrote to us:

I'm old enough that I remember a time before word processing. I would type out papers from beginning to end, drawing just on a sense of how I wanted things to go. But now, for anything longer than an email, my style is modular [flexible]. I break up the project into a series of sub-sections (or chapters, if it's a book), and then work on them in parallel, bouncing back and forth depending on my mood. (I use a program called Scrivener for this—an excellent product.) Often, I don't decide how the sections are ordered until the very end.

Whether going the "straight and narrow" or "jumping" around, writers like you need a sense of the structure of a piece before they sit down to work. A provisional structure—however it guides you—keeps your writing tightly constrained around your thesis, around your argument, around your audience's desires, fears, and needs.

INTRODUCTIONS

To this point we have not talked about how exactly you are going to put pen to paper or words on a screen. This has been intentional. You have to read in the right way first, get ready to ask strong analytic questions about your reading, take a few shots at forming hypotheses to answer these questions, and then understand how to construct an argument. But now is the time to think about the writing out of a compelling argument, which will begin by learning how to craft a good introduction.

An introduction does not—as many high-school teachers instruct—have to be a single opening paragraph. The length of an introduction depends on the length of the essay or article that you are writing. Depending on how long the essay is, the introduction might be two or three paragraphs, but a helpful rule of thumb is that it should exhibit a certain anatomy and form. Every effective introduction has to inspire. This means that very early in a paper you need to break through the absentmindedness and inattention of an audience. Audiences do not come fully loaded to listen undividedly to your every word. The introduction needs to grab a reader's attention and force them or, more gently, encourage them, into reading the body of the essay. An introduction also needs to inform. You need to tell your reader about the topic and the stakes of the argument you are about to make. And every introduction needs to prepare. You want to explain, in shorthand, what you will try to accomplish in the course of your essay. So, remember: inspire, inform, and prepare.

The style of the introduction depends on the content and style of the class you are writing in, or the venue (online magazine or academic journal) you are trying to publish in. But in every case, writing a good introduction is absolutely essential, since it is the "first date" between yourself and your reader. Make a good impression, or it is very likely that your audience will discard your essay in the file cabinet known as the trash can. Don't let this happen. What we are about to work through is the four-part anatomy of an introduction. There might be exceptions to this blueprint, but it has seen us succeed through many years of writer's block, so we want to pass it on to you.

Hook

"I am sorry, everyone. Don't be scared. You are going to die."

This is the first thing out of John's mouth when he teaches Introduction to Philosophy. The class takes a collective gulp, a few nervous laughs escape a few particularly anxious students, and most of them, even the inattentive ones, sit more or less at attention. This is the "hook" for a class about philosophy and the meaning of life, and figuring out how to live well before we die. The opening line of class serves as the "hook," to pierce the inattention and distraction of students on the first day of a new term.

Most readers are ready to be bored and distracted. Your hook is the chance—made or lost in the first one to three sentences—that convinces your reader to stay with you and your argument. It should not, under any circumstances, be the thesis that you eventually defend. It is a teaser, a way of prompting initial thought, or anxiety, or wonder, in your reader about the topic you want to take up. Most people are a little frightened by their own death. They don't think about it much, but when they do, they secretly want a little guidance, or at least a little companionship. To announce, from the outset, that the end is near often prompts students to think about how to make good on the time that they have left, and wonder if there might be some wise thinkers who could be their companions in life's journey. Of course, this is getting close to the "thesis" of the class: "I will argue, as Plato does, that the point of philosophy is a preparation for death, by figuring out how to live a better life." But John does not come out and say it right away. No, he makes the students think for themselves about a problematic, and potentially jarring, hook. Not every hook has to be a matter of life and death. You can use humor ("I always thought I would be in the room when my wife got pregnant"), or historical narrative ("On the evening of 1680 something happened to the British Crown Jewels that would never happen again"), or interesting quotation ("Freedom," according to poet Robert Frost, "is the power of being bold"), but in any event, the first moments of an essay must "pop," creating space for readers to be surprised, perplexed, challenged, or all of the above. Try to imagine the theses with which these hooks are associated.

When you write your hooks, make sure that they are closely related to your thesis, and observe the following suggestions:

1. It should be relatively short.
2. It should get a reader into the mindset of your question, the question that will drive the paper.
3. It should prompt leading thoughts.
4. It should hook into a reader's own life and mind, into a reader's fears and desires.
5. It should be the initial promise to a reader: "I promise you, dear reader, something cool is about to happen."

And try to avoid these dangers in hooking an audience. Avoid:

1. *A generality*: "Since the beginning of time, humans have thought about all sorts of things." What is this essay going to be about? No clue.
2. *Background*: "To understand the invention of Twitter it is necessary to grasp the competitors at the time." Boring.
3. *A cliché*: "In the Gold Rush of 1849, shovels were selling like hotcakes." What are hotcakes anyway? And why did they sell?
4. *Throat-clearing*: "Before providing an original interpretation of *Moby Dick*, it is necessary to first address all of the alternative interpretations." Get to the point.
5. *Specialized language* (make no assumptions about a reader's specialized knowledge): "In Hegel, self-consciousness is the self-revealing of Spirit to itself and opens the way to the life of *Bildung*." What the . . . ?
6. *Stating your thesis at the outset*: "I will argue that W. E. B. Dubois provides an original interpretation of the Black

experience in America that resonates closely with the Black Lives Matter movement." Alright, but don't you want to say something that really gets a reader's attention before getting to the argument?

Motivation

Once a reader has been hooked, they are already on their way to being motivated to read the rest of the essay. This being said, you can lose your reader very easily, so it is necessary to show (rather than tell) them why they should be interested in the way the hook leads to a claim about the intellectual content. So, the hook sentences should lead into a segment of text that deepens the motivation for the essay, about why writing it and reading it is so urgent, interesting, or important. How, you ask?

Remember that the thesis that you plan to advance is the answer to a good question, one that perplexes you and hopefully perplexes a reader. One way to deepen the motivation for an essay is to restate, or make explicit, the question that drove you to write in the first place. You can go back to your reading notes and find the analytic question that you are trying to answer. Imagine posing the question to your reader in a way that makes the question burn for someone else like it did for you. Then write out the problem in clear and compelling language. Keep it to three or four sentences for an eight-page paper.

Another effective mode of motivation is to provide concrete details about the topic that you plan to cover. If you are going to talk about slavery in the United States in the 1830s, you want to make sure that your reader receives some concrete stories or firsthand accounts that demonstrate why the issue is so important and deserves close examination. Even incredibly academic treatments of history, sociology, and economics can open with vivid stories that ground the argument in a real-life event. Tell the motivating story, but don't let it control your whole introduction. It is the preparatory step to expressing your thesis.

Thesis

Now that you have the reader's attention, it's time to lay that thesis on them. Note that the thesis is the third moment of an effective introduction—not the first—and you have grabbed your reader's attention and then given them reason to care about the question or problem you are attempting to resolve. They are now ready to evaluate for the first time your answer. But be careful: there is a danger of saying too little or too much.

In expressing your thesis, you always run the risk of revealing too much, or in other words, making the argument in the introduction rather than in the course of your paper. Don't do this. A thesis is a provisional answer to an important question. Provisional means before things come into view fully. Another way of saying this is that your thesis needs to begin to show what your paper is going to be about, the opening moment of a dramatic unfolding that will be your paper.

Where should a thesis be placed in an introduction? Most professors instruct that it should come at the end of the first paragraph or at the very end of the introduction. And it can, but we would suggest that you embed it in the second half of the introduction, but not exactly at the end of the opening. Remember that the thesis needs to emerge from the motivation of the paper, the question that you set out to answer in the course of the essay.

Methodology

Now that we have some sense of how to craft an outline, let's consider crafting a "mini-outline" for your introduction. That is the fourth moment of your introduction, and it is typically referred to as the "methodology" section of a paper, in other words, the *method* or approach by which you will support your claim. If your thesis gives the "I will argue X" in reference to a question, your methodology, the next step in the given introduction, announces "This is how I plan to argue X." This can be done in very rough outline, especially for a short paper, but we think it should be done in some way.

So, in developing the methodology section of your introduction, ask yourself the following questions:

1. What texts am I going to use?
2. What other scholars will I be responding to?
3. Am I going to use a particular method (or kind) of investigation?
4. Is there going to be a particular order that must be kept in laying out the argument?
5. Is certain context necessary before laying out the premises or evidence?

You might not have the answers for all of these questions, but surely a few of the above will guide you to think of possible responses. Those ideas about the use of texts, the current critical debate, the particular method of inquiry, the order of argumentation, and the context of the claim—all of those ideas should be included, in a very rough outline form, in a few sentences in the introduction. Any of the sentences answering these questions will be sentences pertaining to the methodology of the paper, and give a blueprint for the reader to follow in the course of reading your paper.

There is another "secret" reason you will want to write out a few sentences on methodology in the introduction. In medieval times, some people believed that our bodily movements were controlled by a little being who lived up in our skulls. You and I moved—waved, smiled, and walked—when this tiny being waved, smiled, and walked. These beings, called the homunculi, were the "mini-mes" that controlled us much like puppet masters. Think of the methodology section of your introduction in the same way, as a little homunculus. The methodology lays out the order of events that will take place over the course of your argument. If you ever get lost in writing, you can always return to this methodology to figure out what step comes next in the argument. It is also a promise to your reader about what they should expect. And now it is your task to make good on the promise.

In your methodology, you can gesture to the order of the essay that is going to be read. If you write your introduction first—which is what we suggest (against those that think an introduction can be an afterthought)—it gives you pointers about how to begin your body paragraphs and where transitions might be required in between them to get through them. Make sure that the final sentences of your introduction chart the way ahead into your first body paragraph.

THE MECHANICS OF STRUCTURE

Our instruction to make the final sentences of the introduction "chart the way ahead" into future paragraphs would be rather unhelpful if we didn't say just a little bit about grammatical mechanics. Structure depends on the logical relationship between sentences, between paragraphs, and between sections of an essay. But it also relies on particular words to express this relationship such that audiences can quickly "follow you." Well-written essays aren't just a pile of words on pages. Instead, they're a crafted collection, each word and paragraph lending support and color to the author's ideas. So, a few words about transitions, topic sentences, and signposts: the writer's tools for establishing these well-crafted collections.

Transitions

Transitions help readers, who cannot occupy your mind, follow your thoughts. Better yet, transitions help *you* follow your own thoughts in a smooth and coherent path and progression. In this subsection, we'll consider two classes of transition: (1) words and phrases; and (2) questions and answers.

WORDS AND PHRASES

To finish up, this very sentence starts with a terrible transition into this section, since we're only just starting out on this section: "to finish up" is more of an end-of-section thing to say, something to signal that we are transitioning out. Starting with "to finish up" is dizzying. But ask yourself why we might be dizzied and disoriented by these three simple words. Fourthly, here is yet another confusing transition, since we find no "firstly," "secondly," or "thirdly" to guide us to this "fourthly." Are you lost? Therefore, transitions matter.

Transitional words or phrases glue together bits of writing. These transitions are a special kind of glue: golden glue. In the Japanese art of kintsugi (金継ぎ, "golden joinery"), when a piece of pottery breaks, the broken pieces are glued together again with resin and gold dust. The fractures become golden veins, proudly highlighting the "imperfections" of these broken objects. So lovely is the look of those golden veins that people have deliberately shattered their ceramics so that they could be repaired in the kintsugi style. We think that a critical thinker and writer should play something of the kintsugi artisan and treat transitional words and phrases with the same care and golden dust.

Transitional words and phrases may be categorized in several ways, but we like to categorize them with a "meta" acronym: TRANSITIONS.

- *Time*: sometimes, before, during, after, recently, contemporaneously, etc.
- *Rephrasing*: in other words, stated differently, in simpler terms, this may translate as, etc.
- *Addition*: additionally, also, moreover, etc.
- *Noting*: note that, notice that, noticeably, consider that, remark that, etc.
- *Sequence*: next, firstly, subsequently, finally, etc.
- *Importance*: most importantly, equally importantly, least importantly, critically, etc.
- *Theorizing*: it appears that, it seems that, apparently, perhaps, as if, as though, etc.
- *Inference*: therefore, because of, due to, on account of, since, for that reason, etc.
- *Opposition*: conversely, on the contrary, in spite of, and yet, etc.
- *Narrative*: we could argue that, one might think that, some have suggested, etc.
- *Similarity*: similarly, likewise, identically, equally, correspondingly, in the same way, etc.

This list is not exhaustive, but we hope it provides you with, via all of our examples, a growing familiarity with this golden glue. But what if you need more than mere words and phrases? What if you need full sentences, or something more . . . conversational?

QUESTIONS AND ANSWERS

Why should you keep reading this section? What do you hope to learn? What is the point in us asking you these questions? We suspect that you kept reading because you're a good learner, and that you hope to learn (sooner rather than later) how writers use questions and answers to link ideas and move from sentence to sentence and paragraph to paragraph. Our point, finally, is just what you see here: we've transitioned into our subject using questions and answers.

How often should you use question-and-answer transitions? This depends, but the general consensus of popular writers seems to be "use sparingly" or "use with caution." Why? As you may feel yourself from this paragraph and the previous one, too many questions can annoy a reader. Do you remember what the ancient Athenians did to that relentless questioner Socrates? They executed him.

Still, a good question can get you where you want to go in a paragraph. Sometimes you need to ask questions on behalf of your reader, so that your reader can understand why you're saying what you're saying. Instead of the more laborious "I should explain why birds poop white, because you may not know," you can just ask and answer: "Why do birds poop white? They don't. They pee white. Their poop is that dark stuff that accompanies the white urine, since birds urinate and defecate from the same outlet."

Let's end with a more sophisticated example, this bittersweet bit of solace from the German philosopher Arthur Schopenhauer:

> How foolish it is to regret and deplore the fact that in the past we let slip the opportunity for some pleasure or good fortune! *For what more would we have now?* Just the shriveled-up mummy of a memory. But it is the same with everything that has actually fallen to our lot.[3]

---

3. Arthur Schopenhauer, *Arthur Schopenhauer: Philosophical Writings*, trans. Virginia Cutrufelli (New York: Continuum, 1994), 25.

For what more would we have now? That question is beautifully positioned to carry us into the bittersweet fact that,
good or not, all past moments are reduced to something
bloodlessly abstract. So, what more would we have now?
Nothing more than a slightly higher or slightly lower heap
of ashes. You cannot keep past pleasures, so don't fret if you
missed some. Is this cold comfort? Perhaps.

Topic Sentences

Topic sentences usually appear at the beginning of paragraphs and sections of a given piece of writing. When you
develop a topic sentence, you want to determine the scope
of the text that you are introducing (am I introducing a
short paragraph or a three-page section?) and modify the
sentence accordingly. This is to say that one of the two primary jobs of a topic sentence is to preview what is about to
happen in a given paragraph. You want to give your reader
a clue—at the outset of a paragraph—regarding its content
and message. The second duty of a topic sentence is to recall and gesture to what immediately precedes it. In other
words, you want to reread the previous paragraph and
make sure your topic sentence serves as an effective bridge
between what came before and what is about to be expressed. Below is the rough and ready typology (all the different types) of topic transitions. You will notice that some
are more transition-y, and some are more topic-y. You get to
pick what works best for you in a given situation.

Provide a simple transition: Just like it sounds: closely
related paragraphs don't always need complicated transitions or topic sentences. A simple one will do the job.
"Othello's arrogance might be excusable were it not for his
total ignorance concerning the darkest turn of fate."
Straightforwardly, the previous sections outlined his arrogance, the forthcoming section his ignorance.

Establish a similarity or contrast: Building out an argument of similar premises relies on your stitching different claims together to make a unified whole. This is a topic-transition on Gorman's "The Hill We Climb": "The difficult journey toward racial equality, articulated in Gorman's poem, has an early precursor in Sojourner Truth's lecture, the utterances of a woman who is at the base of Gorman's 'hill.'"

Provide a temporal or spatial transition: It will frequently be necessary to transport your reader through time and place to make a good argument. "The treatment of POWs in the Civil War was not a one-sided affair: the Confederate war prisons in South Carolina were just as brutal as Union internment camps in Delaware." This establishes a similarity and makes a spatial transition.

State a new question to be answered: Essays are driven by the questions they set out to answer. Opening a new paragraph with a related, yet novel, question is a nice way to keep things moving. "Given the discussion of increasing temperatures across the globe, who will be affected first or most harshly by global warming?" This question carries a reader from a discussion of context and background to a pressing practical matter.

Command a reader's attention to take note: You are trying to take your reader for an intellectual ride to deliver them to your conclusion. There can be more or less explicit moments of this ride. A topic sentence might provide the opportunity to be especially forceful. "Notice the stark difference between the Cubists and the Impressionists of earlier generations." This "notice" is a forceful command that insists that the reader take careful note of something.

Provide a framework for elaboration: Certain paragraphs and sections attempt to express a number of related ideas. These are complex paragraphs that occasionally deserve a complex sentence that maps the various ideas for a reader to anticipate. "Given this broad discussion of contemporary cognitive neuroscience in the United States, it is now possible to place the topics of neural reentry, mirror neurons, and bio-feedback in their proper scholarly context." A reader now knows that there will be three topics expressed in the coming sentences. The stage has been set for a complex paragraph.

Express a general statement to be refined: General statements, expressed in simple or slimmed prose, can often open a paragraph by providing something to be refined or elaborated on. They serve as the untouched rock at the outset of sculpting, which an artist molds over the course of a session in the studio. "The summer of 1823 was the cruelest season New Englanders had ever seen." The rest of the paragraph will refine this general claim: why and how this "year without a summer" was truly brutal.

Introduce an example: Certain paragraphs are meant to illustrate general claims. These sections need to be set off by a topic sentence that speaks to that purpose. "Thomas Bradley, a homeless veteran living on the streets of Lowell, Massachusetts, spoke directly to the challenges faced by citizens in the clutches of the opioid crisis, commenting. . . ." This sentence draws a reader's attention from a general cultural or medical trend and challenge, to the particular effects it has on a specific citizen, presenting an effective example.

Signposts

Closely related to transitional and topic sentences is something known as a "signpost." This writerly tool, when used correctly, stands as a logical traffic sign at different places in an essay, and directs a reader's attention forward or

backward into other sections of the text. A signpost can remind a reader about different parts of your thesis at any
moment in your essay; it can gather a set of information expressed much earlier in an argument that needs to be re-
called; it can create expectation about what will sooner or
later be realized or revealed; and it can help you define the
scope of your argument over the course of an essay. Signposts typically are not inserted into the middle of paragraphs, but rather appear at the beginning or end. Some
examples:

> "The treatment of the Kiowa tribes in Kansas in the
> aftermath of the Civil War echoes Lepore's discus-
> sion of the Nashoba in King Philip's War, mentioned
> earlier in the context of early colonial interactions
> with Native peoples."
>
> "There is, of course, an alternative interpreta-
> tion of the events of September 11, one that will
> be addressed later in this essay, but first let's go
> deeper into the angle of vision assumed by the Bush
> administration."
>
> "As we already mentioned, blue jeans have the
> advantage of durability, but now it can be seen that
> cargo pants are both durable and roomy in ways
> that jeans can never be."
>
> "In earlier moments of this discussion, I sug-
> gested that Elmo's appeal might turn on his distinc-
> tive voice as well as the ambiguity and universality
> of Elmo's gender and ethnicity, but now it is clear
> that the exact nose-to-eyes ratio, which reflects
> Fibonacci proportions, explains his astounding
> popularity."

Even gloriously bad arguments can have great transitions and employ effective signposts and make a weak

argument appear stronger than it normally would seem. This is not a particularly noble aspect of rhetoric, but it is true nonetheless. And it is good for you to remember.

EXERCISES

1. Have you already forgotten about hooks? (Did we hook you just now?) Using the lesson on good hooks, write five hooks for five imaginary essays. Pierce through a potential reader's inattention. Create suspense. Prompt wonder. Jar your reader. Wake your reader up!

   Example hooks:

   (i) The earth is flat, at least for a subatomic neutrino traveling directly toward the earth at near the speed of light. For the speedy earthbound neutrino, the earth is more of a squished disc than a spheroid.

   (ii) Americans do not elect their presidents. Electoral colleges do.

2. Using our TRANSITIONS acronym and the examples of transitions provided there, write one sentence for each type of the eleven transition categories, from "Time" to "Sequence" to "Similarity." At the end, you should have eleven sentences. If it helps, you can use any and all of your hook sentences from the previous exercise as sentences from which to transition. Feel free to keep it simple. Consider one our favorite examples of a hook plus transition, which comes from a science article by Katherine J. Wu in *The Atlantic*: "Grizzly bears are mostly vegan. But humans made them more

carnivorous."[4] Wu's pivot from a brilliant hook (the article's headline) to an intriguing thesis is done using one of the simplest transitions, "but," a transition that fits across several of our TRANSITIONS categories, including addition, noting, and opposition. Wu kept it simple, short, and sweet.

---

4. Katherine J. Wu, "Grizzly Bears Are Mostly Vegan," *The Atlantic*, January 10, 2024, https://www.theatlantic.com/science/archive/2024/01/grizzly-bear-california-carnivore-meat-eating/677070/.

Chapter 4
THINKING THROUGH OTHERS

AUDIENCE

The English philosopher and mathematician Alfred North Whitehead once remarked, "[An author] really writes for an audience of about ten persons. Of course, if others like it, that is clear gain. But if those ten are satisfied, [they are] content. A certain amount of encouragement is necessary."[1] Whitehead's comment on the importance and nature of having—and pleasing—your audience strikes us as more or less correct. Whenever we write, even if we write in our journal that remains locked away, we write for others.

And every author has a particular kind of reader in mind, individuals who will understand and appreciate their article, essay, letter, post, book, or whatever. Whitehead hoped for ten. When John writes a letter to his mother, his magic number is one. Our friend Clancy Martin, the author of the recent bestseller *How Not to Kill Yourself*, reflected that anyone writing a popular book with a major publishing house usually hopes for ten thousand. The magic number of readers will be fitted to the type of writing that you envision doing. This community of readers will have particular needs, expectations, fears, and desires, and it is your job as an author to anticipate and speak to them clearly.

---

1. Lucien Price, comp., *Dialogues of Alfred North Whitehead* (Boston: Little, Brown, 1954), 66.

In the author-audience relationship, it is easy to think that the author is the one in the driver's seat. After all, the author is the one guiding their audience through the various moments of a text. Wrong. The audience is always in charge, because a reader, at any moment, has the power to set the text aside and find something better or more satisfying to peruse. A philosopher-acquaintance of ours once made the rather harsh suggestion that authors should assume the worst of their audience as being "stupid, boring, and rude." She contended that this perspective encouraged authors to write in simple and compelling ways. We respectfully disagree with this acquaintance. An author should assume that a reader is *free*—that is all—and that this freedom implies that a reader can, and will, turn elsewhere for information and inspiration if you don't convince them to read to the end. Human life is incredibly precious because it is incredibly short, so it is ill-advised to waste a reader's time.

So, who is your audience? And how should you think about them?

Who Is Your Audience?

Audiences come in different shapes and sizes, but the most important question you need to answer is whether your audience is known or unknown. Known audiences include readers you personally know or those who have needs, expectations, fears, and desires that you can anticipate easily and accurately. Maybe you are writing an essay on the ethics of drone warfare—as John once did—and know that it will be read by military officials who employ drones all the time and advocate their expanded use. What will they expect and need in an argument? What assumptions can you make about their knowledge and stance? If you can answer these questions about your reader, they are part of a known audience. The audience most known to you is, naturally, yourself; all the notes and journal entries you make are tailored to your needs, expectations, fears, and desires, and you know them as well as anyone.

Unknown audiences are much trickier to address because you never know—nor even could guess—how they will interpret a given piece of writing. Unknown audiences are much more common than known ones as you advance in your writing career. You might get to know your professor in the course of a class, but when it comes to your first submitted essay, they constitute an unknown audience of one. If you write an essay for the SAT or another standardized test, you will never know who graded your piece of writing. For most students, this is a rather frightening unknown audience, but it doesn't have to be. You just have to ask the right questions about the readers who might come across your writing. The next section, entitled "Thinking about Your Audience," will help you get a better sense of even the most obscure unknown audience.

An audience is not one uniform thing, like a bowl of oatmeal that is roughly the same gloopy stuff throughout. The audience for most popular essays is actually a conglomerate of multiple audiences, consisting of many readers with very different points of view. In this case, an author needs to anticipate the dissimilar interests of all parts of an audience. An author writing on the use of psychedelics in treating women who have suffered severe trauma could envision speaking to the following groups of readers: (1) those interested in the research surrounding psychedelics (for and against); (2) those interested in women's psychology and physical health; and (3) those interested in post-traumatic stress disorder. All of these cohorts will have slightly, or very, different perspectives, and an author wants to make sure that she develops her thesis and motivates her essay in light of these views.

Thinking about Your Audience

When we talk to a friend, we tend to acknowledge who they are and what interests they have before we open our mouths. This can be a conscious effort, but it usually happens so quickly and automatically that we fail to notice it. Thinking about your audience for a piece of writing is not nearly as natural, so over the years we have developed a series of questions that help us get a better handle on known audiences and anticipate the view of unknown ones.

1. *Whom do you want to reach?* First determine whether there are multiple audiences who might take an interest in your thesis. If so, you will want to do some thinking around identifying their age (or age range), gender, socioeconomic class, geographical location, and educational background. It's OK if these are rough estimates. Remember that just because you want to reach a certain segment of the population does not in any way mean that they will be the only ones to come across your writing.

2. *What exactly interests readers about your subject or thesis?* Next, you need to anticipate the particular stance your readers might have on the topic at hand. Why do they want or need to spend their lives thinking about the subject?

3. *What does your ideal reader already know about the topic?* Do you know more or less about the topic than your average reader does? Which kinds of readers know the most about it? Which ones are new to the topic?

4. *Where do your readers usually get their information?* You will need to determine whether your writing style and form fit with the typical information a reader finds reliable about a topic.

5. *Is your reader likely to agree or disagree with you?* Try to figure out which segment of your audience will accept

the various aspects of your argument or story as plausible. Why do proponents of the argument already agree? Do you need to restate these reasons in your draft?

6. *What are the greatest obstacles your reader faces in agreeing with you?* For those readers you know or anticipate will be skeptical, from what do their doubts arise? You will want to think about the sharpest and most critical reader in your audience so you can take measures to speak to their concerns.

7. *What counterarguments could be used to face these obstacles?* What counts as compelling evidence to your most skeptical readers? Your arguments—posed to convince this segment of the audience—must draw on this sort of evidence.

8. *What would you like a reader to do, or feel, about your essay?* Essays can evoke great emotion, create context for future research, or directly impact decisions and actions. You will want to envision the consequences of your writing on an audience. What is to be done, once a reader reaches your conclusion?

"Do you buy my argument?"

This is a standard question we hear when eavesdropping on student peer-review sessions. It reveals an important analogy between marketing a product to be bought and constructing an argument to be believed. Recently, we asked the chief marketing officer of a *Fortune* 500 company about writing marketing copy for an audience.

"Our readers are customers," she began. "You have to show them that the squeeze is worth the juice."

There is a cost in time and effort in reading anything. You, as a writer, need to make sure that the reward of working through your written words is "worth it" for a reader. Our marketing friend put a point on the importance of

Get to Work

IMAGINE YOUR AUDIENCE

Imagine you plan to publish three thesis-driven pieces, and two of them you hope to publish in "big name" publications: *Psychology Today* and the *New York Times*. The editors of these publications will want to know "Who is this for?" Describe three possible audiences for each of the three pieces.

1. A three-page essay in *Psychology Today* with the thesis "I will argue that the nineteenth-century philosopher and author of the *Principles of Psychology*, William James, provides concrete guidance for parents trying to raise kids who are prone to violent outbursts at school."
2. A 1,200-word op-ed in the *New York Times* with the thesis "I will argue that the rise of far-right organizations in Europe in the last ten years jeopardizes the basic principles of the European Union."
3. A 1,000-word personal essay on addiction and yoga with the thesis "I will argue that yoga saved my life by helping me overcome life-threatening addiction."

fitting her message to the particular disposition of an audience.

"Buyers have specific fears and desires," she continued. "You have to show that your product, and only your product, is best fit to address them."

In business, this is called a "value proposition," the simple summary of why a customer should choose your product or service over any other. It should articulate the benefits that a customer will receive from your company, and why no other company could supply this value. Now, a similar thought process needs to take place as you craft a piece of writing for an imagined audience. You must envision the pain points and desires of your reader and—at least in your own head—be able to articulate why your essay, and no other essay, provides something necessary and unique to your "buyer" (we mean, reader). This is a key to writing for others.

COAUTHORS, MENTORS, AND PEER REVIEWERS

Sometimes you need some guarantee that another human being will actually read this little thing you are spending so much of your life creating. The silent covenant that you make with yourself before writing anything—namely that you promise not to destroy it in the end—is simply not enough to prevent self-sabotage. On these occasions, the loneliness of being a writer is more intolerable than usual. This is why we frequently write with others. Sometimes you become a coauthor because you can't stand writing by yourself.

In her novel *The Blind Assassin*, Margaret Atwood wrote, "Perhaps I write for no one. Perhaps for the same person children are writing for, when they scrawl their names in the snow."[2] Perhaps she's just wrong about this. Many children may scrawl their names in snow—and in sand, on dirty windows, bathroom stalls, and old desks—with the secret hope that someone will take note. At least some of these children go on to become writers whose feverish scrawling disproves the fear that all of it will go unacknowledged. If they go into the humanities, as we did, this fear may never go away. If we are really honest, we'll acknowledge that it's this fear that drove us to write with

---

2. Margaret Atwood, *The Blind Assassin* (New York: Anchor Books, 2001), 43.

others, and to write this very short section in praise of coauthors.

On the Virtues of the Coauthor

All writers write in response to the writings of others. We write for communities, if only imagined ones. Sometimes we acknowledge this communal work and call it collaboration. But in some writing contexts, you might call it professional suicide. Little has changed since Aristophanes wrote *The Clouds*, in which Socrates is portrayed as floating high up in the clouds of worthless philosophical speculation. Real writers and thinkers, the type that get famous, are supposed to fly their intellectual balloons all by themselves. But maybe the point is not to be famous, but to put out the most compelling piece of writing as possible. And that requires a little help at times.

To be clear, it's not easy. After all, we have to find someone who wants to write with us. And then there is the small issue of our not playing particularly well with others. This isn't exactly the same as disliking others, but we've usually been the kids writing our names in the snow while everyone else went sledding. This is complicated by the odd nature of academia, where playing well with others by being friendly in your correspondences as opposed to hostile can seem weak, or expressing yourself in a way that others can understand you, as opposed to being difficult, can seem simple-minded. Such are the norms of many (misguided) academic disciplines. But sometimes the risk of appearing weak and simple-minded is better than complete irrelevance. Of course, finding a good coauthor doesn't mean that you won't be irrelevant or that you will want to go sledding with everyone else.

Scholars working in the natural or social sciences will find all of this ridiculous. They have, for centuries, collaborated in productive ways on the most relevant issues of their day. And so their disciplines, as a rule, are not on the verge of extinction. We are not suggesting that cowriting in the humanities can save some fields from this fate—we suspect it will take more than this—only that writing *with* others might be a first step in writing *for* others.

At least it was for us. Finding coauthors was our first intimation of a world beyond what David Foster Wallace describes as each person's "tiny skull-sized kingdom."[3] Writing with others involves giving up absolute power over the subjects of our little kingdoms, a type of power that some solo writers spend their whole lives attempting to maintain. In many fields of study, the number of possible topics for a writer seems painfully small, and the intellectual realm uncomfortably narrow, so being forced to give up your dominion might feel like a bit of a cosmic injustice. But in the end, coauthors have helped us see that we were giving up next to nothing in sharing this so-called power.

So, what is it, precisely, that a coauthor gives you?

1. *Coauthors catch the things you can't remove by yourself:* your blind spots, your stylistic tics, your unfounded assumptions, your implicit biases, your inelegance, your vagueness, your repetition.
2. *They give you the opportunity to bounce your half-baked ideas off another*, and this sometimes results in the creation of something completely new, something that neither of you could have come up with on your own, like a song featuring multiple artists.
3. *Coauthors can release some of the pressure and anxiety surrounding the process of writing.* Some days you won't know how to write the next section, or which logical

3. David Foster Wallace, *This Is Water: Some Thoughts, Delivered on a Significant Occasion about Living a Compassionate Life* (New York: Little, Brown, 2009), 117.

connection to make, or how to conclude an essay, and so on. This is where the joys of coauthorship come in. Your collaborator can and often does come to the rescue, completing a writing task that you just can't stomach.

4. *While coauthors aim to write for the same audience, they also provide a fresh perspective on the audience you want to reach.* You might think that you know your reader, but your coauthor probably thinks the same thing, and if you talk it out, you are most likely to have a better sense of your general readership.

5. Writers often assume a certain voice and style, which is perfectly fine and normal. But it can become repetitive. *Coauthors, at their best, enliven the writing and formal expression of a given coauthored essay with a unique blend of voice and style.*

Finally, coauthors can serve as mentors whom you regard with something like reverence. If you choose wisely, your coauthors can become your teachers in the art of writing and the conventions of a particular genre or discipline. In other words, coauthors often serve as writing mentors, indispensable figures in your writing life.

Finding a Rhetorical Mentor

To write well, you need to learn from those around you who already do it. You need the help of mentors. You can do this in your interaction with senior coauthors whom you know very well or with famous authors you might never meet. There are a variety of mentors available to you—and you should make the most of all of them.

1. *The mentor, known and unknown:* When you read, you usually do so to glean certain content from the words: you look out for what information serves you and ig-

nore, for the most part, what does not. We tell our students, however, to read not only for content but for style and form. In other words, how does the author put a piece of writing together? What grammatical constructions are used most often, what serves as an effective introduction and topic sentence, what sort of transitions are used, and what is the tone and argument of the piece? This line of questioning will reveal a way of writing that you may choose to adopt in the future, and provide templates for essays should you ever find yourself at a stylistic loss. You may never actually meet the authors you admire, but you will know their writings inside and out.

2. *The famous potential mentor, once contacted*: Writing is a lonely business. Even the most famous writers (with some exceptions) look forward to getting feedback on their work. So, reach out to your heroes. Many writers will have academic appointments and university emails that you can find rather easily. For the elusive few, you will have to read the acknowledgments of books or articles, and contact a writer's agent to pass along your note (they almost always do). Now, how do you get a potential mentor to respond to you? First, in an opening of no more than two sentences, make clear who you are and what you aim to write or think about. Then pose a question regarding the content of the author's work, ideally observing a place in the argument where more work could be done (without accusing her or him of missing something), and suggest that you might like to work on this area of research. Finally, compliment the author on something you like about the work, and make clear that you would really appreciate a response about the above question. And then make it easy for them to contact you; include your physical address, phone number, or email. Even if this writer never

responds, time has not been wasted. You have tried to get into the action of a critical debate directly, and you should be applauded for having the guts.

3. *The sort-of-famous, teacherly mentor*: You look up to some of your teachers for good reason: some of them are amazing writers. There are conventions, stylistic choices, modes of research and reading, and tricks of the publishing trade that they can pass down to you quickly and easily. And they would love to. You want to start with the line of questioning used in approaching the famous writer, but you also want to set up a meeting or time to talk on the phone or by video chat as soon as possible. You need to read their work carefully and have several strong analytic questions about it to show the author that you are invested in the conversation. You also want to have three, and no more than three, working theses that are closely related to the writings that you admire. Now, if this potential mentor is a little rude or too busy to meet right away, give them a little time and don't take it personally (scholars can be a bit cagey about their time). Persist and insist a little bit, without being rude yourself. If nothing comes of the interaction, go find another sort-of-famous writer to chat up—there are plenty of those fish in the sea.

Ideally, this sort of mentor will ask you to help them in their next scholarly or writerly pursuits, while, at the same time, teaching you the ropes of style, voice, form, and research. "What could I, a literary newbie, contribute to a well-established writer?" Quite a bit, it turns out. You might be asked to support the mentor in gathering citations, or taking reading notes, or doing field research, or simply talking through ideas. This is an invaluable experience that most writers have had at one or another point in their early lives.

4. *The publishing, editing mentor*: We will talk about peer-review and the editing process in a second, but we want to say just a couple of words about all the wonderful people who work in publishing and editing. And how you might use their wonderfulness.

If you think that writing is a lonely pursuit, you should talk to some of the editors of academic writing. Their desks are stacked high with manuscripts, and they often prefer just about anything to working through more of them. This means that these are prime people to talk to about the process of publishing and editing. Say you come across a stellar academic article in the field of medieval English or an op-ed in your local paper that you utterly adore. Most likely, there is a great editor behind those pieces of writing. Reach out to them (usually authors will be happy to put noncrazy strangers in touch with their editors). So, act uncrazy and ask for the contact. Then have three, and no more than three, interesting questions about the piece, and about writing more generally, that the editor or publisher could address.

PEER REVIEW

The most common experience of "writing with others," at least in the context of a student's formal education, will be in what is known as a peer review, in which you exchange draft writing with another student and provide editorial feedback. This interaction can be useless and frustrating, but it can also be invaluable and enjoyable. The difference lies in knowing how to give and how to receive constructive criticism.

When you start to review a draft, as a peer editor, you want to make a charitable first reading: read the draft without looking for things to correct. Try to understand what the author is trying to convey, what information is being used, and what ideas are driving the essay forward. After finishing, ask the author what they would like you to focus on. Perhaps the author already knows the thesis lacks clarity. Perhaps she already sees something amiss with the use of sources. As editor, you should concentrate on these difficulties first in your peer review. As you begin the second reading of the draft, write a letter to the author on a separate piece of paper. You can write comments—both positive and negative—but make sure you lead with something you like about the draft first. Instead of merely circling things that aren't working, make sure that you provide suggestions and alternatives that the author can use directly in the revision process. Avoid generalities in criticism: "I don't like this section." Instead: "I think this section would be more effective if you moved the source materials on urban planning to the first paragraph." Make sure you can speak to the following aspects of the author's draft:

1. Is there an analytic question? What is it and is it motivating for the reader?
2. Is the title of the essay an effective and interesting one?
3. Does the introduction function to inform, inspire, and prepare a reader adequately?
4. Does the introduction reflect proper anatomy: hook, motivation, thesis, methodology? Is the thesis clearly stated and compelling?
5. Is evidence used effectively in the service of this thesis?
6. Has the author met your expectations and needs as a reader? Who is the ideal audience?

7. Do phrases or key terms need to be defined?
8. Does the essay conclude in a satisfying way and in a way that reflects the author's purpose?

If you can answer these questions, you will be able to provide very useful feedback to an author. But what if you are the author? How should you receive feedback?

Criticism should be delivered respectfully and carefully. Criticism should be received in a similar manner. Don't quibble with your reviewer or get defensive. This is not the time for that. If she didn't understand something in your essay, that is your problem, not hers. Even if you think that everything is crystal clear, it is worth a second look. Take notes on your reviewer's comments. This will occupy your time if you have the urge to argue. It is always a good idea to assume that criticism is given "in good faith," meaning that your reviewer is trying to help you, not hurt you. This doesn't mean that criticism doesn't usually hurt—it does—but that is not the reviewer's intent. Community is necessary for good critical thinking. It is hubris—excessive pride—to think that you do not need guidance in your first steps into a foreign land. Only an arrogant little stinker rejects the knowledge of others because "I wish to prove or disprove everything myself!" You need to get help. How do we know this? Because you are reading the words of two one-time little stinkers who discovered the error of their ways.

An advanced critical thinker knows that they depend upon other advanced critical thinkers in countless ways. Critical thinking can backfire on you if you aren't critical of your own abilities. So, admit that you are a human being like the rest of us and not a little god. Admit that there are others who know better than you on countless subjects. Admit that you're probably wrong about more things than you think you're wrong about. Good critical thinking—not just any old critical thinking—is done in a tradition and community of researchers, not with four Google searches.

Still have doubts? Imagine that you stumble upon a human skeleton in the middle of a hike. Of course, there are some safe assumptions you could make. For example, "This looks like a skeleton." Apart from that, since you're not a forensic *anything*, any further conclusions you puzzle out, even guided by your critical thinking, will be far less reliable; in fact, they will be almost wholly unreliable. Did the person die here or were their remains put here? Was the person killed? What was the age of the person? Your critical assessment is probably less than worthless (that is, if anyone used it in a trial, the trial would be a fiasco). It is OK to admit that you're not a forensic pathologist (unless, of course, you are a forensic pathologist). Most of us, for better or worse, are not forensic pathologists.

Now imagine that someone among us calls up the authorities. They arrive and you insist to them, based upon your "careful avoidance of fallacies" (such as straw man and false alternatives), that the skeleton was of a forty-year-old man who was murdered by arsenic and whose body was placed here by the murderers (yes, plural; there *must* have been two murderers, or one murderer and an accomplice, since the victim was too heavy to carry for one alone). You would be rightly dismissed, even rightly laughed at. Why? Well, the primary critical error you made is hubris, that classic tragic flaw.

Peer review is an institution that short-circuits hubris by forcing authors to submit their writing to a panel of experts before it is accepted to an academic journal or made into a scholarly monograph (which is a book about one academic subject). If you want to be published, you send your manuscript to the editor of a journal or publishing house, and then they hire (or just beg) experts in your field to evaluate the writing. It is a daunting but incredibly important process in every academic field of study.

Peer Review at Its Best

Since peer review depends on the thinking of others, we asked some other professors what they thought of peer review. One of them was John Traphagan, a professor of religious studies at the University of Texas at Austin. "The most important aspect of peer review is that it provides a system for vetting research to make sure it's of high quality and academic integrity is maintained in published work," Traphagan said. But he wasn't finished:

> Additionally, peer review creates a broad framework in which, even if the reviews are blind, there is a collaborative element to the dissemination of research results. Edits and comments from reviewers represent an important contribution that often significantly improves both the content and writing of an article or book. Good reviewers can pick up on errors in reasoning, problems with writing, and mistakes that may lurk in how data are interpreted. In short, peer review keeps researchers humble.

It is very hard to be arrogant as a scholarly writer for very long. Some thinkers pull it off, but not many. Peer reviewers serve as the gate-keepers of academic periodicals. Some journals have a very low acceptance rate, because they accept only the most rigorous, original, and motivating articles. To the extent a journal selects for rigor and originality, that journal shows us peer review at its best.

Peer Review at Its Worst

In our conversation with Traphagan, it became clear there were also potential dangers regarding the system of peer review. "The most significant danger of peer review," he explained, "is that it can stifle innovation and creativity. Reviewers are often resistant to work that pushes their field in significantly new directions or challenges established ideas within a discipline. The peer-review process has a way of putting the brakes on work that is risky and significantly different from established conventions of research and academic writing." Peer reviewers are always selected on the basis of their expertise. To achieve expertise, one has to write a great deal about a particular subject, and put forward unique interpretations on that topic. Reviewers—like all authors—can become wed to their own views (and resist those of others), and they can develop an allergic reaction to submitted papers that run in the face of their cherished interpretations. This means that such a reviewer will not approve strongly countervailing positions, and the journal, therefore, will lack a diverse or wide breadth of possible interpretations. It happens. This is always a danger in the peer-review process, but it is a danger worth facing given the significant benefits of peer review.

As a reader-researcher, you should know how peer-review operates in the context of the periodicals, books, and articles that you are using as sources. Check the journal's website to find the editorial board, the submission guidelines, and the acceptance rate (not all journals make this information public). This will give you a pretty good idea of the "who" and "how" of a publication's peer-review process.

EXERCISES

1. Would you like to have an audience for the things you write? Why or why not? And if you would like an audience, who would you want in it? If it helps to think through, write for a couple of minutes about this. Or discuss with a writing partner.

2. Who are your mentors? From authors you've never met to teachers who have helped you, list your mentors and a sentence about why they have fit that role for you. If you have difficulty listing your mentors, or would prefer not to, then write a short paragraph about how you might go about finding mentors. What steps could you take to find good mentors? Whom could you ask? Where might you go? And what qualities would you most want your mentors to possess?

3. In your own words, briefly describe how you see the difference between "constructive" and "nonconstructive" criticism. Using the description you just wrote, come up with a possible reason why some people choose to use "nonconstructive" criticism instead of "constructive" criticism. Finally, for people who do choose "nonconstructive" criticism, what "constructive" criticism would you offer them?

Chapter 5

THINKING THROUGH THE SELF

THE "I" IN WRITING

When we write, we have the chance to express ourselves and to make our mark. When we write, we also have the chance to review our own thoughts and get to know ourselves. This may sound mawkishly sentimental (another way of saying "cheesy"), but it's true. One way to keep writing fresh and interesting, one way of making writing a lifelong practice, is to find yourself in any set of words you put down.

At the beginning of *Walden*, published in 1854, Henry David Thoreau makes what he assumes is a bold admission: "In most books, the I is omitted, in this it will be retained." Today, in our age of selfies and oversharing, this remark sounds quaint. Ours is the age of memoir—both serious and trivial. There are, however, intellectual disciplines in which use of the "I" is still deeply distrusted. Writers who dare to use personal pronouns in these disciplines risk being criticized. But over the years, we have come to think that while the risk may be great, so too—sometimes—is the reward.

Why include the "I"? After all, one is directing their writing, whatever it happens to be, to "you," the reader. If an author thinks what they are writing is true of human beings generally, they can do so without reference to their own personal experience; and if what an author is writing about is completely strange to their own experience, it is at least a bit bold and perhaps downright rude (and maybe worse, downright boring) to talk all about it in the first person. "Nobody wants to hear about you," John's grandfather, a salesman, used to say, "but anyone will pay you to listen to him talk about himself."

This might be correct, but occasionally authors can, and should, speak explicitly for themselves. This lesson has spawned a subdiscipline of anthropology, autoethnography, in which an author employs introspection to understand and present a cultural or social phenomenon. But this approach has been slower to catch on in history, philosophy, and literary studies. There are, however, several notable exceptions.

Some lessons are learned best through example and demonstration. This is probably one of them: there are a variety of ways in which first-person, personal writing and memoir can be effectively integrated into academic writing. Let's consider a few.

The "I" in Academic Studies

In 1992, Nicholson Baker wrote *U and I*, a short confession of his love-hate relationship with the writer John Updike.[1] Baker offers interesting vignettes of Updike, but, more importantly, a sense of how a truly famous author touched a (somewhat jealous) contemporary. Indeed, Baker and Updike share many things—most notably, a meticulous attention to detail and fluid prose—and we get to know Updike's writing better, and more intimately, as Baker gives us something of himself. In short, Baker's sometimes-embarrassing personal approach gives us Updike as he understands him, which is to say, as a semineurotic fan understands him. Fast-forward nearly twenty years, to the

---

1. Nicholson Baker, *U and I: A True Story* (New York: Random House, 1991).

publishing of *Out of Sheer Rage: Wrestling with D. H. Lawrence*, Geoff Dyer's memoir about not writing a book about D. H. Lawrence.[2] Dyer's procrastination and ambivalence about the project—expressed as an incisive memoir about the nature of art and writing—reveals the hidden Lawrence, the one reflected in partial (unfinished) manuscripts and insane (but meaningful) misadventures. And Janet Malcolm's brilliant metabiography of Sylvia Plath and Ted Hughes, *The Silent Woman*, simultaneously interrogates two lives while struggling openly with the best way to do so.[3] Malcolm is "right there" with Plath and Hughes to the very end. All of these authors produce genre-transgressing works: biographies about writers, by writers, writing about themselves. Or memoirs by writers, writing biographies about other authors. Take your pick.

The Pulitzer Prize-winning Megan Marshall took this memoir-cum-biography approach in her original study of the American poet Elizabeth Bishop, entitled *Elizabeth Bishop: A Miracle for Breakfast*.[4] Marshall won the Pulitzer Prize for her traditional biography of the nineteenth-century philosopher Margaret Fuller, but she didn't always want to write nonfiction. In the 1970s, as an undergraduate at Harvard, she wanted to be a poet. Elizabeth Bishop was her teacher. So, Marshall broke protocol, made like Thoreau, and used the "I," developing a biography with two narrative lines—a central stream that details Bishop's life, and another written in the first person that occasionally flows into the central current.

2. Geoff Dyer, *Out of Sheer Rage: Wrestling with D. H. Lawrence* (New York: North Point Press, 1997).

3. Janet Malcolm, *The Silent Woman: Sylvia Plath & Ted Hughes* (New York: Knopf, 1994).

4. Megan Marshall, *Elizabeth Bishop: A Miracle for Breakfast* (Boston: Houghton Mifflin Harcourt, 2017).

In a recent conversation with us, Marshall acknowledged the risk she was taking in writing this sort of book. In the discipline of history, women continue to be marginalized, both as subjects of history and as authors who are worth citing, and this may extend to women authors' willingness and ability to interject themselves, as male authors like Dyer and Baker have, into the biographical stories they wish to tell. In other words, not only is there always the possibility of being perceived as self-indulgent, but this particular hazard is greater, perhaps far greater, for women authors, who traditionally have been dissuaded from including their narratives in the arc of history. Marshall, however, took the risk and produced a book about how poetry can emerge from life, or rather from two adjacent lives.

"I can't imagine doing anything quite like this again," Marshall admitted, after the reviews from the *New York Times* and *Harvard Magazine* criticized her book for including personal anecdotes about her time with the poet laureate.

> The situation was unique—I don't have any other subjects like this up my sleeve! That same uniqueness, though, made me feel this was a book I had to write, was destined to write. It came as a gift, as all biographies do—the gift of the subject's diaries, letters, published work. But in this case, there was a matching gift in my own life experience, lesser but important to me, and that I believed would amplify Bishop's essentially tragic life story (except for the miraculous poems that came out of it).[5]

---

5. Megan Marshall, email message to author, March 2017, cited in John Kaag, "Putting the 'I' in Biography," *Literary Hub*, March 22, 2017, https://lithub.com/putting-the-i-in-biography/.

Marshall made it very clear that her own story was second-ary to Bishop's, that one of the real dangers of writing this way was to mistakenly allow one's sense of self to dominate the subject at hand. Personal, first-person writing can make its way into an academic study, but it should only do so when there is a very good reason, when it provides mo-tivation, evidence, or a compelling demonstration of a for-mal thesis.

Point of View in a Rhetorical Stance

College writing instructors have been known to forbid their students from using the "I" in their writing. The under-lying reason for the prohibition? Students occasionally confuse personal opinion ("I think Socrates is stupid") and defensible position ("Socrates's use of irony in the Platonic dialogues is not an effective way of teaching because it often drifts into mere hypocrisy"). In our experience, the worry concerning this confusion is overblown. Authors can express baseless opinion without using the "I" and also form powerful theses by including it. We think it is better to take one's cues from Mark Claddis, head of religious studies at Brown University, who has occasionally taken personal approaches to academic topics. Claddis remarked,

> We are trained to impart only a highly limited, spe-cialized portion of what we have come to know and understand. There are good reasons for respecting these boundaries, lest we fall into indulgent nar-cissism, self-therapy, or presenting our personal doctrines and stories as "The Way." Still, there are occasions when we should be willing to offer some-thing beyond our specialized training—not neces-sarily more of our personal lives (though that may be appropriate at times), but certainly more of our

wide-ranging reflections and narratives about what we have come to find significant, troubling, horrific, or beautiful.

When an author sits down at her desk to write, she is trying to express something that she has found "significant, troubling, horrific, or beautiful." That is also to say that she is attempting to express her unique point of view. An author's point of view is an essential aspect of her argument, discussed at the outset of the book, the unique way a writer approaches a particular topic. In formal academic writing, the point of view remains merely implicit, the trace of a person beneath the thick veneer of argumentation. In personal writing, however—the sort that Thoreau, or Marshall, or Dyer produced—this point of view was made explicit and a focal point.

This is crucial to remember when it comes to employing the "I." What is your objective? Thoreau was attempting to demonstrate how the principles of American Transcendentalism, developed in the 1830s, might shape the practical affairs of a man's life, namely his life. Marshall attempted to create a harmony between two lives, that of a teacher and student, which was more powerful than either narrative read in isolation. Dyer revealed his point of view to explain just how absolutely frustrating another author could be to a contemporary reader. Sometimes talking about yourself is just egotistical, but sometimes it can reveal something momentous to a reader that would remain hidden in a more objective account. So when should you reveal yourself in your academic writing? Here are some conditions under which to consider using "I" language:

1. *In the introduction of an essay by telling the story of how you first became interested in the topic.* In other words, use it

as motivation. "If I am interested in this, I think you should be too." If you open with the personal, you might be able to close with it as well in your conclusion.

2. *If it serves as a case study.* If you are writing about urban blight in Chicago, and you were raised there, personal narrative might go a long way to supplement your evidence.

3. *If it tests a theory.* If you are studying the principles of Christian monkhood, particularly the practices of fasting as they emerged in the early church, and if you have fasted seriously yourself to test these principles, it makes sense to share the story.

4. *If you have changed as a person in accord with an argument that you are discussing.* Making your reader feel the life-changing power of logic, through your own experience, can be extremely compelling.

5. *If you have conducted field research, especially with human or nonhuman subjects.*

6. *If you need to be implicated in the argument.* Controversial arguments are often made very compellingly by recent converts to the position, especially if they reveal earlier positions that they held.

Determining when and how to effectively reveal yourself in writing is an ability that is honed over a lifetime of practice. You will make mistakes, we promise. John's editor at Farrar, Straus and Giroux, Ileene Smith, recently told him that she had spent the better part of her career toning down his self-revelation. "Don't reveal *so* much, John," she said. Less is often more when it comes to personal writing. But an attempt can be made. At the end of the writerly day, human beings are storytelling animals, and they love to hear tales about other humans—including stories about you and me.

INTEGRATING YOUR INTERESTS

"This writing assignment is *so boring*."

Trust us: no writing assignment is *that* boring. Working on an assembly line, packing boxes on a truck in the middle of summer, valeting cars in a public parking lot, picking strawberries for five hours—this stuff is boring (we know from experience). Writing is always potentially interesting, because you always have the opportunity to integrate your particular interests into an assignment.

If you are interested in soccer but have to take a philosophy class, ask the professor about writing on the philosophy of sport. If you are musically inclined but have to write an analysis of material design in an engineering class, ask the professor if you can write about the construction of the cello. There is almost always the space in classes, and certainly in writing, for what might be called creative integration: the combination of your preexisting passions and the writing prompt.

Ten years ago, John met an eighteen-year-old student in his Ethics of War and Peace class at Harvard Extension School. Her name was Enal Hindi, a young woman whose family had emigrated from Palestine to Chicago to, in her words, "escape the violence." Her father worked at Mr. King's Gyros on 71st and Halsted. When Enal submitted her final essay for the class (prompt: "please analyze some aspect of human rights violations in armed conflict in the last 40 years"), she wrote that her father had escaped the violence and injustice of war only to be murdered three years later in the United States for one hundred and twenty dollars. Having revealed her point of view, she went on to argue that refugees who flee human rights violations in war zones are often forced into the poorest communities, wracked by violent crime. The writing was so simple, so powerful. There just needed to be more of it. Over the next three years, Enal and John met every month—to expand the essay, to hone her craft, to amplify the beautiful voice she had discovered. The essay was published in *Harper's Magazine* as "Allah Knows" in 2017.

Enal's story is not only a remarkable case of a writer revealing her point of view, but an instance in which a student integrates her experiences into a formal academic assignment, and in the process became a truly powerful writer. It should also be a point of inspiration: You can do this; you can write vibrantly and find your voice in an essay prompt, if you are willing to be honest about what already thrills and frightens you. "Enal is just an English genius," you say. No. Enal's first language is not English. She is a self-described "science nerd," but she became one of the best young writers in the United States by plumbing her experience and understanding the relationship between introspection and argument. Introspection, the process of looking at yourself—and in the context of writing, figuring out what makes your story or argument distinctive—is an absolutely crucial step in becoming an author. *Author* comes from the Latin verb *augeō*, "to originate." Many of the best authors allow their writing to originate in their lived experience, and then explain the wider significance of this experience in the context of history, theory, and culture.

Working Out Your Interests

OK, OK, enough of the grandiose talk. Let us provide a few practical exercises that might help you take your experience and interests seriously as the starting points of thinking and writing. Find a partner and talk openly about the following questions:

1. Name one or two of your favorite classes, and describe what your favorite lesson was in each and why.
2. What do you like to do in your free time? Describe in detail the reasons you find it significant.
3. What was the scariest moment of your life and what fears do you still have, and why?
4. What are you really good at—like so good that you could teach someone else the skill?
5. What do you like to read and why?
6. What is the proudest moment of your life and why?

Don't worry: this isn't group therapy (we are not qualified for that)—just the chance to express the inner reasoning of your interests. This inner reasoning of your passions will often resonate with, or be related to, the topics in many of your college courses. Maybe you love to open-water swim or spend time at the beach, and you read Thoreau's account of traveling to Cape Cod only to find his experience was interestingly different from your own. Or maybe you read *Lord of the Flies* in high school and you absolutely loved it—and now you see that this riveting story reflects some of the principles that you are forced to learn in your social and political philosophy class. This insight—about the connection between a book you like and some theory that you really don't—might be the first step in integrating your vivid interest in a future assignment that at first strikes you as tedium itself.

The "I-Search" Exercise

Another way of situating yourself in the context of formal academic research is not about connecting a personal interest to a discrete thesis, but rather about doing research on an aspect of your identity. The exercise that you will undertake is known as the "I-Search Exercise" and was introduced to us by Eileen Pollack, the former head of the

Get to Work

KNOW THYSELF

First, pick five possible topics about yourself that you would like to learn more about: your family history, your hometown, your favorite food, how your parents met, where your father went to college, what happened to your long-lost aunt Greta. Anything, really. But pick five possible topics. With the help of a peer, pick one of these topics and formulate a central analytic question (usually a how or why question) that you are intent on answering. If your interest is in the origins of your family (the topic), you will want to narrow to a manageable question: "How did the prohibition of alcohol affect my family who lived in the border regions of Canada and the United States?" You will want to ask some related questions: "How much of the family was involved in bootlegging? How wealthy did they become from the sale of alcohol? What was life like for the women of the family? Who were the most notable and historically significant families in the area, and how did they live?" Finally, and perhaps most importantly, engage in what is known as "metacognition," a reflective move where you ask about your own motives in the investigation: "Why am I interested in this topic?"

writing program at the University of Michigan, but it was first developed by Ken Macrorie in the late 1990s. The sense of urgency and interest in writing and reading can be lost in formal composition, so Macrorie structured a paper prompt around a student's interests about themselves. In "I-Search," a twist on re-search, students look for answers to questions about themselves, search for evidence to support these answers, and reflect on the method of inquiry and the findings of their investigation.

What will this investigation yield? That is largely to be seen. Our student Janice asked about how her parents met in college. Her mother was Jewish. Her father was Catholic. She discovered during I-Search that at that time it was taboo for Jews and Catholics to date, much less get married. And she discovered in the college archives a stock of letters to a local paper—written by her parents— protesting the inhibiting cultural norms of their time. Janice had no idea about this, but after the I-Search project she thought about her family and herself in a whole new way.

Macrorie suggests that students construct a research paper in three stages: (1) describing the search itself; (2) defining and examining the search results; (3) reflecting on the meaning of the search results but also on the search itself.

1. *Describe the search.* Catch a reader's attention and interest; explain why learning more about this topic was personally important for you. What did you already know and what did you assume? Show a reader why she or he might also be interested in the investigation. What are your central question and four related questions? Describe in detail the steps that you took in the course of your investigation. Be honest with your reader about what was hard and what was straightforward in the search. Foreshadow the key findings of your search.

2. *Examine the results of the search.* Provide the findings of your search and give the evidence that you employed to support these results. Use direct quotations, summary, and paraphrase to give your readers a clear picture of your evidence. Properly cite all your source evidence.

3. *Reflect on the search.* Discuss what you think is most meaningful about the results and what you learned from your research experience. How have you changed

your mind in the course of your research, and how will you act or think differently given this search experience?

THE PITFALLS OF THE PERSONAL IN ACADEMIC WRITING

The I-Search project is a perennial favorite among students. Why? When else do you get to make yourself the focal point of a paper, research some charming aspect of yourself, and call it classwork? In the course of your I-Search, you might sense the potential disaster in integrating your personal life into your writing: you can easily get carried away. We are all self-centered little beasts, just by virtue of how we experience the world as essentially "mine," and we enter dangerous territory if we begin to let this fact dominate our writing. We can express ourselves in writing, but it should rarely be for our own sake, but for the sake of being understood by others.

Avoiding Insider Terminology

We mentioned the shortcoming of jargon earlier, the way that specialized or disciplinary-specific language can be used to confuse, rather than clarify, the message of an author. Something similar can occur in your personal writing when you assume that a reader understands you as well as you might understand yourself. "When my brother called me *dappich* on the soccer field it hurt my feelings." Unless you were born near Lancaster, Pennsylvania, and grew up surrounded by people who spoke Pennsylvania Dutch, you won't have the faintest idea why John's feelings were hurt. Maybe his brother was calling him smelly? Or too loud? No. *Dappich* means clumsy, which is precisely what John was. In using terms that only a fraction of people understand, or that only he understands, an author asks too much of a reader. He has essentially short-circuited the possibility of communication.

Avoiding Arrogance

"My thesis on the virtues of swimming is reflected in my own life in which I made deep and lasting friendships on my relay team that won three national championships and vaulted me into a million-dollar modeling contract, where I met my model and brain surgeon of a spouse."

We just threw up a little bit in our mouths. Arrogant first-person narrative is about the worst sort of writing imaginable. It's off-putting, alienating, and contentless. Just. Plain. Awful. You want to establish your expertise as an author, but you never want to make a reader feel insecure and resentful, much less powerless and stupid. Think about your audience as a bunch of well-meaning loose acquaintances. They aren't your family and friends, who are happy to listen you brag. They are thoughtful people who expect to be treated thoughtfully.

Humble-brag—boasting masquerading as self-effacement—is no better, and in some cases worse, than straightforward, arrogant self-assertion. Avoid both.

Avoiding Taking Oneself Too Seriously

"I am arguing in a long and illustrious line of authors including Lord Byron, Ralph Waldo Emerson, and Henry David Thoreau, all of whom held that the worst thing in life that one could do is waste it. We have repeatedly argued that you should follow in our footsteps, into the beauty of the natural world to find the meaning of life."

Foolishness. You might be a good writer, but it's likely you can't hold a candle to Byron, Emerson, and Thoreau. And even if you could, you wouldn't say as much. This isn't just a matter of arrogance, but rather of taking yourself and your argument too seriously. The experiences that one has in life can feel so vividly real, that it is easy to confuse them for being magnificently important. "I was heartbroken; this was the worst betrayal in the history of the world, and now the world was ending." Probably not. It just felt that way—and a reader will be able to see something you fail to recognize, namely that you have lost perspective. Try to keep an eye on overblown assertions while in the personal mode. They are almost always signs that you are mistaking your experience for greatness. Experience should be honest, authentic, real—never expressed as being overly grave or serious. Of course, some experiences *are* serious, but stick to the facts and let your readers be the judge of that. If you are worried about coming across too gravely, you might consider a little bit of self-deprecation, our favorite trick to humorous writing. To err is human, so to show yourself in error is to show your reader that you are human. And readers almost always like deeply human authors who reach for something like authenticity.

Avoiding Inauthenticity

Don't pretend. A reader will know, almost immediately, if you are pretending to be someone else. Write clearly about the matters you find vitally important. We asked an expert on authenticity, Skye Cleary, a professor of philosophy at Barnard College, to define authentic writing. She responded,

> An authentic artist, according to Simone de Beauvoir in *The Second Sex*, "will go beyond the given in the way she expresses it, she will really be an artist, a creator who gives meaning to her life by

lending meaning to the world." The same applies to writing, including academic writing. Certainly, a writer must acknowledge the given, that is, the academic framework and context in which they are working. But an authentic writer pushes against and beyond these boundaries in their expressions and methods to reveal new truths, meanings, and perspectives both for themselves and others.

It is tempting to hide behind the conventions of a particular type of writing or genre. Everything seems so safe and formulaic. But safety sometimes comes at a high price— the price of expressing something of yourself in clear and compelling prose, which can be handed to untold readers for years to come. Dare to say it in your own words, in your own way, according to your own understanding!

ANXIETY AND WRITER'S BLOCK

Why Does Writing Provoke Anxiety?

In May of 1818, seventy-five-year-old Thomas Jefferson wrote a letter to John Adams, in which Jefferson moaned, "My repugnance to the writing table becomes daily & hourly more deadly & insurmountable."[6] When he felt hostile to the act of writing, he would read:

> In place of this has come on a canine appetite for reading. And I indulge it: because I see in it a relief against the *taedium senectutis* [the weariness of old age]; a lamp to lighten my path thro' the dreary wilderness of time before me, whose bourne I see not.

---

6. "Thomas Jefferson to John Adams, 17 May 1818," National Archives and Records Administration, accessed January 4, 2024, https://founders.archives.gov/documents/Jefferson/03-13-02-0042.

Losing daily all interest in the things around us,
something else is necessary to fill the void. With me
it is reading, which occupies the mind without the
labor of producing ideas from my own stock.[7]

Jefferson wanted to fill the void with words, just not his
own words. Many writers know this predicament. The void
whispers to us: "All your writing is pointless" or "You're a
mediocre writer." The void is cruel. We'd rather do something else, anything else, than fight the silence with our
own words. The void stabs us again and again as we sink
into silence: "Who would even read your writing?" "This is
just a stupid journal entry." "This assignment is a waste of
time." "You are no Hemingway!" "You've tried and failed so
many times; just relent." The void has suffocated us many
times. Calling it "writer's block" makes it sound tame, as if
it were merely about writing. The void swallows you whole;
the writing is merely one part of you it swallows—the part
that can scream.

Screw the void. Don't listen to it. Make it listen to you.
The authors of this book scream at the void frequently, to
refresh ourselves from a bad week, or worse. As professional screamers-at-the-void, we have some advice on how
to scream when you feel the silence, and the inner criticism,
overwhelming you.

What Is Writer's Block and How Do I Deal with It?

Lower your standards. That is the advice of the American
poet William Stafford for defeating writer's block.[8] We
think Stafford's advice works wonders, when taken to
heart. Lowering your standards means caring less about

---

7. "Jefferson to Adams, 17 May 1818."

8. William Stafford, *Writing the Australian Crawl: Views on the Writer's Vocation* (Ann Arbor: University of Michigan Press, 1978), 118.

the quality of your writing. Writing poorly may be a counterintuitive recommendation in a book about writing well, but writing poorly is the open secret of writing well. To get to good writing, you go through the muckiest of crummy writing. In other words, experts in good writing are also experts in bad writing.

So, how do you lower your standards? We suggest what another American writer, Charles Bukowski, suggested: "Writing about a writer's block is better than not writing at all."[9] Write about why you might feel blocked. Just start with a "nothing sentence," a sentence that is more like babbling than writing: *I got writer's block like nobody's business.* Then, just blurt out another sentence: *Writing is the worst.* Then, blurt out another sentence: *Is this even a good sentence?* Don't think about what you're writing. Don't care about what you're writing. Just *blah-blah-blah* it. Let your standards sink lower and lower until they totally disappear into a bottomless pit of *blah-blah-blah*. Nothing matters down here in the word-abyss. Just babble away as you fall.

Eventually, after a paragraph or two or three of babbling, something stupendous might happen: You might start to cozy up to what you're writing. You start to feel OK. Your words and your thoughts start to feel indistinguishable, as if you're writing *exactly* what you're thinking, without much fuss and anxiety. Baby step by baby step, your babble becomes prose. It may not be the best prose, but who cares? This is about unblocking words, not judging words. This is personal, not professional. This is time for baby talk, not Shakespeare. You can always delete your baby talk and act as if you never needed the help of such nonsense (as sometimes we pretend that we were never screaming,

9. Charles Bukowski, *The Last Night of the Earth Poems* (New York: Ecco, 2002), 194.

crying, barfing little babies, but were born as fully matured adults). We were all babies once, and sometimes we need to be babies again.

But suppose you've tried baby talk for several pages and still—still!—you feel blocked up. Somehow the babbling fails to mutate into prose. Somehow the baby never grows up. What do you do then? Well, on the far side of infancy is death, so try a deadline.

A deadline, like death, robs you of an infinite future in which you can do everything *later*. It pressures you to act like a mortal, alive for a mere blink of time and then *poof* gone forever. Yes, this fatal knowledge (of death and deadlines) can create stress, but this stress can be good stress, what psychologists call "eustress" (from the Greek prefix "eu-," meaning "well" or "good"). Eustress is positive and creative stress, not the negative stress that freezes you up and tears you apart. Eustress excites and inspires. Think of the eustress of planning a trip abroad. Despite all the hassles of airplane schedules, hotel prices, museum hours, emergency plans, and luggage, passports, and bank cards, etc., etc., we still thrill at the fun little vacation details. *Oh, let's dine there! Oh, let's book a room with that hotel on the cliff!*

A deadline, ideally, creates sufficient eustress to get you to the finish line. Of course, most deadlines are not like travel planning; they're not fun. So, we should make them fun. When you create a deadline for yourself (or when you're *gifted* a deadline by a *charitable* teacher), attach a celebration to it. Dine at your favorite restaurant. Shop at your favorite store. Go to a musical performance, nature park, or art museum. Whatever it is, make it special, truly. Treat yourself. But please, only celebrate *when* you meet your deadline. If you celebrate prematurely, your brain, like the brain of so many opportunistic mammals, will remember how easy it is to avoid the blackberry thorns and gobble up all the blackberries.

Finally, deadlines can be divided into easily digested smaller deadlines: "microdeadlines." For example, suppose it is Monday and you give yourself the deadline of writing 2,000 words by Friday. Below is a possible microdeadline schedule.

Monday: 100 words
Tuesday: 250 words
Wednesday: 250 words
Thursday: 400 words
Friday: 1,000 words

This schedule back-loads the work; Monday is light, but Friday is a nightmare. This may work for you. Or you may want to front-load the work, and coast breezily into a light Friday. Some of you might be even Stevens and wish to do exactly 400 words per day. Trust us, though, you will likely renegotiate these word counts with yourself several times during the week, so don't worry too much about the hard numbers. Aim for approximations. Some days you will write fewer words and some days more, but always try to get close to your microdeadlines. The only hard number you should respect is the one promised at the final deadline (the deadline which, when met, you celebrate).

Of course, dividing word counts is not the only way to create microdeadlines, but it is a clear and quantitative way of chunking work. You could chunk work by page count or, more trickily, by percentage of your outline completed (see chapter 3's section "Outlining"). In whatever way you chunk your work, be realistic with yourself. Consider your body's need for rest and distraction. In fact, your body, as we'll discuss in the next subsection, should be considered more generally in all creative tasks.

How to Manage Creative Anxiety in General

One word: self-care. Self-care is a suite of self-soothing behaviors that nourish a sense of control and tranquility. Self-care techniques often focus on the usual source of our problems: physiological states. Thinking and writing are unavoidably physical. Long hours of sitting and reading, or sitting and writing, can have adverse effects on our bodies. The sedentary and mostly isolated process of "thinking through writing" is hard on the body, so one remedy is to go gentle on the body. We're serious. Anxiety is psycho-physiological, so psycho-physiological methods are needed. But since we're not psychiatrists, and since we don't know you at all, and thus cannot diagnose anything, we won't recommend prescription anti-anxiety drugs, but we will come close.

Lavender is one of our personal "prescriptions." Lavender calms. Clinical studies of an essential oil extract of *Lavandula angustifolia* have shown it produces a calm without sedation, dependence, tolerance, or withdrawal. It may seem odd to find a recommendation for lavender in a book about critical thinking, but critical thinking, it must be repeated, is not divorced from the nervous system. The *bodily* process of critical thinking is often ignored in the literature, but that, in our opinion, is comparable to ignoring the topic of audiences in critical thinking; we need to come back down to earth from all that pedagogical idealism. Again, taking lavender is only one of many ways to relax; the point is to find what helps *you* relax. Here, then, are three ways to take your lavender:

1. The most direct method of *taking the lavender* is through a softgel supplement, such as CalmAid. One side effect of lavender softgels is "lavender eructation," aka lavender burps. As a long-time user, Jonathan can attest to the pleasantness of a lavender eructation; it is a breath of fresh lavender air.

2. Drink a cup of lavender-chamomile tea before bed.
3. Sprinkle a few drops of lavender essential oil on your pillow.

On the topic of beds and pillows, our next prescription is good sleep. Your writing and critical thinking will suffer if you don't get good sleep. Good sleep helps your focus, mood, memory, and pretty much everything else you need to operate the heavy machinery of thinking. Four tips, when faithfully followed, will improve your sleep.

1. Don't eat two to three hours before sleep. Digestion competes with restorative sleep.
2. Make your room as dark as possible, e.g., by using blackout curtains. Cut out all light, especially blue light, such as that radiating from smartphones and televisions.
3. Aim to go to bed at the same time every night. Pick a time right now and give your bedtime a special meaning, e.g., 11:11 p.m. (numerical symmetry). Now write down your bedtime and its special meaning. Going to bed at the same time every night requires stick-to-it-iveness, but eventually, with enough repetition, your body will do it for you.
4. All in all, make your bedroom a supremely restful place, whatever that means for you.

Now, both authors of this book are admirers of the nineteenth-century German philosopher Friedrich Nietzsche, who totally smears the line between mind and body. In his autobiography *Ecce Homo*, Nietzsche writes, "Of quite different interest to me is a question on which more 'salvation of humanity' hangs than any theologian's novelty: the question of *nourishment*. A handy way of formulating it is like so: 'How exactly do *you* nourish yourself in order to reach your maximum of strength . . . ?'"[10] Nietzsche would include in "your maximum of strength" your power to think clearly and creatively. Nutrition, aka good diet, is essential for critical thinking, according to Dr. Nietzsche—and we agree.

Unfortunately, in addition to *not* being psychiatrists, we are also *not* dietitians. So, we will keep our suggestions brief and uncontroversial.

1. Avoid or reduce (and if possible, eliminate) trans-fat and high-fructose corn syrup from your diet.
2. Avoid or reduce highly processed foods.
3. Avoid or reduce fried foods.
4. Avoid or reduce foods with sugar or sugar substitutes, such as aspartame and sucralose.

Finally, we recommend short, sustainable, and gamified exercise. "Gamified" exercise simply means exercise made into a game, for example, a team sport or performance; this is exercise that you don't register as exercise. Ideally, you forget you're exercising in gamified exercise. When you neglect the raw utilitarian aims of exercise and think only of winning a tournament or perfecting a toe loop jump (e.g., in figure skating), you are, in a sense, *not* exercising, but playing. The short-term rewards of a game pull you forward into winning, before you know it, the long-term rewards of exercise. Gamified or not, exercise will help you through a creative block. If you want a recommendation for a delightful form of exercise, though not exactly a gamified one, we recommend the Dutch practice of *uitwaaien*, from *uit-* "out" and *-waaien* "to gust (of wind)." Uitwaaien is a light jaunt into oncoming wind, and a wintry wind if possible; the colder the better (within reason, of course).

---

10. Friedrich Nietzsche, *The Complete Works of Friedrich Nietzsche*, vol. 9, *Ecce Homo* (Stanford: Stanford University Press, 2021), 231.

However you manage your creative anxiety, whatever path you blaze to escape your bad weather, we recommend in all cases a unique *style* of travel: the gentle style. The gentle style may be summarized in the mantra "Go gentle on yourself and others." Once more, go gentle on yourself and others. And one final repetition, to make this mantra a lighthouse in your memory: go gentle on yourself and others.

Some prompts to consider for your self-care:

1. What is your favorite relaxing ritual?
2. What is your ideal bed time?
3. What is your healthy comfort food?
4. What is your favorite way to get exercise?

EXERCISES

1. In your own words, describe two reasons that you should consider revealing your point of view.
2. Write a paragraph of whatever nonsense your heart desires for the next five minutes. Just *blah-blah-blah* whatever comes to mind for a paragraph. There is neither judge nor jury here, so go wild and clear away all blocks!
3. When you have some leisure time, sit still and do absolutely nothing for twenty minutes. Just be with your thoughts. Don't read anything. Don't watch anything. Don't listen to anything except the ambient sounds of your world (no podcasts, music, etc.). Some people might call this "meditation," but don't get hung up on that term. Just do nothing for twenty minutes except observe your surrounding environment. This exercise is truly a kind of physical exercise, meant to help you think and write by supporting the thing that thinks and

writes: your body. We want to remind you that you do in fact exist bodily, and that every*body* needs care and consideration. The life of the mind, contrary to what a philosopher like Descartes might say, is indissolubly bound to the health of the body. You think, therefore you thirst, hunger, and sleep—and sometimes, you need twenty minutes of simply existing.

Chapter 6

THINKING THROUGH EVIDENCE

JUSTIFICATION

Let's talk about how to support an argument in that essay of yours.

We make lots and lots of claims; we are confident in some claims and unsure about others. One claim we all feel confident about is that "the sun will come up in the morning." Now, if we were to tell you that we knew this claim to be true because a fortune-teller told us so, or because we just felt it so in our left pinky, you would be reasonable to say that we didn't really know this to be true at all. Our claim about the sun, even though it is true, would rely on bad evidence. This is an example of the difference that philosophers like to make between "true belief" and "justified true belief." In this case, our claims to actual knowledge of the truth depend on us having or not having a justified true belief—that is, a good reason behind our belief. The reasons are what ultimately matter in knowing or arguing for the truth, reasons that can be communicated, evaluated, questioned, and endorsed. And these reasons, when put together, provide the justification. As you think and write, you will constantly reevaluate and reconstruct arguments on the basis of their possible justification.

What Is Justification?

Justification very rarely (if ever) is 100 percent proof of a claim. Practically speaking, justification means presenting the reasons for holding a belief such that a reasonable audience might follow these reasons to reach a similar conclusion. Skeptics since the ancient Greeks have observed that there is a serious formal problem with justification: every claim must be supported by another supportable claim, which in turn must be supported by yet another supportable claim. But this problem of regress should not bother you as a writer and thinker, at least not in any significant practical way. Practically speaking, claims can be more or less justified by reasons, and the trick in your writing is to give your audience *sufficient* (or enough) reason to change their minds about a given subject by either intentionally reinforcing a belief that they may already have or bringing them around to your conclusion against the odds. Justification gives you that power.

Being open to another person's argument on the basis of sound (good) justification has certain virtues that often go unmentioned.

1. Grounding our beliefs in justification should allow us to avoid error regarding a variety of topics.
2. Being open to sound reasons is the key to being a skillful knower (even if you don't know anything for certain). It allows us to be self-critical, receptive, and humble in regard to what we hold true.
3. Being open to convincing reasons means that you are open minded and willing to engage with critical conversation, which can convince you to change your mind. This means that you are not living in a bubble of self-imposed ignorance. Well done.
4. Insisting our beliefs be anchored in sound reasoning is crucial in forming responsible beliefs. Believing without justification is tantamount to holding irresponsible, reckless beliefs.

5. Pursuing reasonable justification in arguments is a sign that you are committed to the great human endeavor of truth-making and to other goods like intellectual well-being, social trust, and the upholding of justice over injustice.

In your writing, you will need to construct arguments: claims supported by justification. You justify your claims with a variety of evidence. Let's walk through the kinds of evidence and how you might employ them.

EVIDENCE

The American journalist and humorist Ambrose Bierce, in his infamous *Devil's Dictionary*, defined "self-evident" as "evident to one's self and to nobody else."[1] Very few claims are universally and immediately accepted, without evidence or justification. A thesis is necessarily controversial, which means that at least a segment of your audience will need some amount of convincing in order to buy your argument. This is where a careful selection of evidence comes in. You will need to judge what pieces of evidence present your thesis in the most convincing light, but also underscore its importance, make it stand out, or establish revealing similarities.

What Counts as Evidence?

In essays in the humanities, evidence is usually unearthed in a close reading of a variety of texts. This is known as textual evidence, segments of readings from primary or

---

1. Ambrose Bierce, *The Unabridged Devil's Dictionary* (Athens: University of Georgia Press, 2002), 213.

secondary sources (meaning original texts or secondary texts written about original texts) that an author employs to reveal something significant about their thesis. In the social sciences, evidence typically comes in the form of quantitative or qualitative data. Social scientists (e.g., anthropologists, psychologists, sociologists), using experimental methods, can attempt to employ quantitative measures, which are converted into numerical values. During the twentieth century, researchers acknowledged that data could not be exhaustively summarized or captured by numerical measures: qualitative research was born. In other words, qualitative researchers assume that words (descriptive, verbal, and story-based) could be used as effectively as numbers to reveal reliable answers to research questions. As George R. Taylor explained, "Data collection [in the qualitative mode] and validation consist of in-depth open-ended interviews, direct observation, and written documentation (i.e., questionnaires, personal diaries, and program records)."[2]

When you deploy evidence in an essay, like marshaling the troops in battle, you will want to make sure that it provides the support that you need for the given context. In other words, you need to envision exactly how you will integrate, or include, evidence in the justification of your thesis.

Integrating Evidence

Including evidence should never be a matter of satisfying a teacher's dull insistence that you "include three sources." They are well-meaning, but that instruction does evidence a bit of an injustice. Instead, integrating evidence is about

---

2. George R. Taylor, ed., *Integrating Quantitative and Qualitative Methods in Research*, 2nd ed. (Lanham, MD: University Press of America, 2005), 4.

recognizing gaps in your argument and gaps in your knowledge, finding the appropriate support materials from the work of others (usually scholars), and then knitting this information into the fabric of your essay. To do this, you will want to quickly acknowledge the specific ways the evidence will be used to establish your thesis *before the evidence is given*, and then explain the significance of the evidence *after it is expressed*. You can use evidence in a variety of ways (that we will go over in the next section on sources) in addition to using evidence as direct support, and you will want to orient your reader to the reasons why the range of your evidence has been selected. Integrating evidence in a transparent and informative way also has the advantage of demarcating what is "yours" and what is not, a helpful first step in avoiding plagiarism.

Summary, Paraphrase, Quote, and Rogeting (SPQ-R)

When you are using another text as a piece of useful evidence, you need to extract and convey the information carefully and with a sense of the audience's preexisting knowledge, as well as the type of source you are using. There are three distinct and valid ways of conveying information from sources. And one very distinctly invalid one:

Summary: The heart of the source, putting it into your own words.

Paraphrase: A piece of the source, but not verbatim and, more importantly, in *your own words*.

Quote: A verbatim piece of the source, in either quotation marks or block text.

Rogeting: Using synonyms to avoid plagiarism-detection software. Still a form of plagiarism.

Summarizing is necessary when you present an entire work or section of that work in a shortened form. It should provide an overview of the entire relevant section of your source, as opposed to just a part of it. A summary should have no more than half the words of the material being summarized. To summarize, give a brief overview of what you are summarizing. Summaries are not long, but the length depends on the importance of the source within your own paper. Ask yourself: at what point will your summary start to distract readers from your purpose? Here's what we advise: summarize when you don't need everything that the author has said—such as examples that don't directly apply to your topic or would take up too much space—when paraphrasing or quoting adds too much length to your text, when you can say it "better" than the author, or when you can use it in a different way.

Paraphrasing is taking information from a source and putting it in your own words without changing the author's intended meaning. It is more detailed than a summary, so it should focus on a single idea and is only slightly condensed. When you paraphrase, be sure to stay true to the source's idea, but also be sure that you're not just making small changes to the sentences, but using different words or sentences to express the same message. You should paraphrase when the information presented by the author would be very difficult for the reader to understand, or when you need to demonstrate your understanding of what the author is saying. To paraphrase, take the author's words and rewrite them in a way that makes sense to the reader. This may be as simple as completely rewording the idea, so it doesn't lose its original meaning, or as complex as integrating the author's ideas with your own to create a new meaning. Remember: small changes to the original sentence(s) are not enough to qualify as paraphrasing.

Quoting should be used when you cannot paraphrase without losing meaning, or when the quote encompasses the main point of what you're trying to convey to the reader. A direct quote uses the author's exact words and is noted by using quotation marks (" "), or set off with a block quote. Because it is directly from the text, direct quotes are the easiest way to use sources, but such use can be deceptively easy, and easily lead to misuses. So it is especially important to use signal phrases ("In *Critique of Pure Reason*, Kant considers a counterargument to his claim: [. . .]") when directly quoting so your reader knows where the quote comes from and how it is framed in that source. Most importantly, you need to connect the quote to the rest of your paper.

Rogeting is a form of plagiarism (we will examine plagiarism closely at the end of this chapter). It is the act of substituting synonyms for someone else's words. This might allow you to avoid detection of plagiarism-finding software, but your professor or an informed reader will be able to sniff out the act of pretending to be someone you are not.

Let's test out SPQ-R and play with an example.

> Some great writers produce a profound effect by their work as a whole, but are not readily quotable; others have the gift of condensing their meaning into a striking phrase. The conscious and deliberate literary artist will generally be found to belong to the latter class. Pope, for example, is the most quotable writer in English after Shakespeare. Stevenson stands intermediate. On the whole, he rather diffuses his meaning, and makes it an atmosphere enfolding everything; but at times his skill in words concentrates itself in a sentence or phrase, or even in a word.
> —Hugh Walker, *The English Essay and Essayist* (New York: E. P. Dutton, 1915), 298.

SUMMARY OF THE WALKER QUOTE

Writers vary in the way their works can be summarized and quoted. Some writers require that readers work their way through a whole passage to capture the meaning, while others provide pithy one-liners to express the meaning of the entire passage.

PARAPHRASE FROM THE WALKER QUOTE

Shakespeare is the most quotable English writer, followed by Pope.

You'll notice that our paraphrase here captures only a part of Walker's quote; it does not give us an overview of Walker's quote, as a summary would. Both a summary and a paraphrase should be in your own words, but with a paraphrase, you don't need to summarize the whole quote. A paraphrase can be a *looser* restatement of *less* of the source material than a summary. A summary sums up. A paraphrase may or may not sum up.

QUOTE FROM THE WALKER QUOTE

As Hugh Walker writes, "Pope, for example, is the most quotable writer in English after Shakespeare."

Notice that our quote is not a summary of the whole passage.

ROGETING THE WALKER QUOTE

Let's *Roget* the first line of our Hugh Walker quote: "Some great writers produce a profound effect by their work as a whole; others have the gift of condensing their meaning into a striking phrase."

Some eminent authors generate an overpowering impression through their writing, when considered holistically. Some writers possess the endowment of distilling their substance into an astonishing locution.

Get to Work

SPQ-R

As you may know, "SPQR" is an acronym for *Senatus Populusque Romanus*, which means the "senate and people of Rome." It is sometimes said that Romans just copied Greek culture with only minor variations. That is not the fairest way to frame the cultural exchanges between ancient Greeks and Romans, but we can still have some fun at the expense of the ancient Romans and use our SPQ-R skills to use a classic Greek text for *our* purposes. Take the following Greek myth and SPQ-R it!

"Why Life Is Hard" by Hesiod (from *Works and Days*)[1]

You know, the gods never have let on
How humans might make a living. Else,
You might get enough done in one day
To keep you fixed for a year without working.
You might just hang your plowshare up in the smoke,
And all the fieldwork done by your oxen
And hard-working mules would soon run to ruin.
But Zeus got his spleen up, and went and hid
How to make a living, all because shifty Prometheus
Tricked him. That's why Zeus made life hard for humans.
He hid fire. But that fine son of Iapetos stole it
Right back out from under Zeus' nose, hiding
The flame in a fennel stalk. And thundering Zeus
Who rides herd on the clouds got angry and said:

"Iapetos' boy, if you're not the smartest of them all!
I bet you're glad you stole fire and outfoxed me.
But things will go hard for you and for humans after this.
I'm going to give them Evil in exchange for fire,
Their very own Evil to love and embrace."

---

1. Hesiod, *"Works and Days" and "Theogony,"* trans. Stanley Lombardo (Indianapolis: Hackett, 1993), 24–25.

As we'll find in the last section of this chapter, this example plagiarizes the author's words by merely switching out some of the words of his quote for other words with the same meaning while not attributing this idea to the original writer.

Explaining Your Evidence, or Evidence in Context

The reasons why you include certain types of evidence while possibly omitting others may be evident to you, but it is usually not completely obvious to a reader. This is why it is so important to explain to an audience the specific justification for the use of evidence; you have to convince the reader that the juice of your sources is worth the squeeze of thinking through them. Remember that *your* reader is supposed to be captivated by *your* thesis, and only interested in an argument or data set employed by another scholar to the extent that it helps justify or frame *your* conclusion.

Of course, you can draw from research with which you disagree, but it should never overpower your central writing goals. Typically, it helps to put evidence in the context of your thesis in the paragraphs immediately preceding or following its usage. Here are a few helpful tips:

1. *Identify for the reader the medium of the evidence.* Is it a letter, a data set, a census report, a scholarly article, a first-person testimony, a court ruling?
2. *Locate the evidence chronologically and culturally.* Is the census report from Minneapolis in 1922?
3. *Mention who produced the evidence and for what original purpose.* Was the letter written by President Roosevelt to his advisor, in reference to the origins of the Cold War?
4. *Identify the role that this evidence is playing in your argument.* This will be addressed more easily after you read the upcoming section on sources and their uses.

SOURCES

In the course of research, you will, in the words of Zora Neale Hurston, do a good deal of "poking and prying with a purpose," unearthing a number of strong sources, and many weak ones.[3] You will need to make distinctions between sources and learn to use them in a variety of ways. The sources you employ will depend not only on the topic you select, but also on the academic discipline you're writing in and the audience you are trying to reach. After selecting and integrating your sources, you should ensure a consistent citation method that allows a reader to evaluate your source materials. All of this may seem painfully dry; we remember a particularly vocal student once telling us that "citations occupy a certain circle of hell." Actually, citations can save you from a very nasty circle of academic damnation.

Evaluating and Using Sources

There are three principal distinctions that you will want to make in selecting sources: first, between reliable and unreliable sources; second, between scholarly and popular sources; and third, between primary and secondary sources.

A reliable source—one that you can rely upon in a particular context of an essay—comes in many shapes and sizes, and its reliability depends on how you want to use it. If you are looking for an informative source, one that can provide conceptual support for an argument, you will want to find a source that has been produced by experts in a field for other experts in a field. If, on the other hand, you

---

3. Zora Neale Hurston, *Dust Tracks on a Road* (New York: HarperPerennial, 1996), 143.

are looking for direct evidence about some cultural phenomenon—like an aspect of social media—you will find popular sources that provide the evidence you are searching for. The difference between a popular source and an academic one is determined not by who produces a work, but rather by who the intended audience is for a text or source. Some scholars write both popular and academic texts, so you need to be careful that you are finding the texts with the scholarly rigor you need.

In high school, you might have heard a teacher talk about primary and secondary sources without having had the nerve to ask about the difference. *Primary sources* are immediate, first-hand accounts of a topic. Primary sources include published books, newspapers, and magazine clippings published at the time of an event; texts of laws and other original documents; articles by reporters who witnessed an event or quote people who did; and speeches, diaries, letters, and interviews (what the people involved said or wrote). *Secondary sources* are one step removed from primary sources, though they often quote or otherwise use primary sources. They can cover the same topic, but add a layer of interpretation and analysis. Secondary sources include most books about a topic; analysis or interpretation of data; scholarly articles or other articles about a topic, especially by people not directly involved; and documentaries (though they often include photos or video that can be considered primary sources). Interestingly, the context of your research often determines whether a given source is to be regarded as a primary or secondary source. For example, Jacque Barzun was a literary critic and historian who wrote a great deal on the American philosopher William James. If you are researching James's psychological research in the 1890s and draw on one of Barzun's essays, the essay would be regarded as secondary. If, on the other hand, you are researching the evolution of Barzun's thought on American pragmatism, the textual evidence gleaned from his essays would be primary.

Here is a rough and ready list of ways to use sources. In each case, you will most likely use a different signal phrase, which orients your reader to the reason for using this source.

For context: The argument you are making never stands in total isolation. Secondary sources, arguments made by other scholars, can present the critical debate to a reader.

Historical setting: Primary and secondary sources can quickly articulate the particular historical timing and background setting against which your argument matters most.

Personal details: Maybe you are writing about Victoria Woodhull, the first woman to run for US president, but you need some texture for your narrative of her early life. In this case, relying on primary sources that describe her family might do the trick.

Cultural trends: If you are writing on the invention of the Internet in the twentieth century, you might want to provide an expert analysis of the rise of the automobile as a metaphor or comparison.

Expert testimony: You might not be one of the leading scholars on German opera of the nineteenth century, but you have been asked to write a paper on Wagner. Time to find the words and opinions of the experts to lend credence to your argument.

Reception of primary materials: Secondary sources can be incredibly helpful to show you—and your reader—how primary materials have been interpreted in the past through the current moment. This information will allow you to find a unique niche in the literature and explain to a reader how you fit in.

For conceptual support: Maybe you are making an argument that we have a moral obligation to treat nonhuman animals with dignity and respect. In this case, you, like Peter Singer, might turn to historical arguments made on behalf of human creatures to set the terms of the argument.

Direct support of the thesis's truth: You are making the argument that the presence of HOX genes in insects explains a given pattern of mutation, but also increases an animal's fitness. If the claim about mutation has already been made, then you are halfway there. Make sure you include these supporting researchers' work as source materials.

Direct support of evidence in body paragraphs: You need to argue, among other things, that the risk of economic inflation slows spending in the tech sector. Another researcher interviewed the head of Amazon in the financial downturn. That interview is a good source for you in your body paragraphs.

Indirect support of theory or methodology: You are taking a new methodological approach to understanding Henry David Thoreau's two-year experiment at Walden Pond by making your own cabin and documenting the experience.

As contrast and counterargument: Dr. Disagreeable has argued against the position that you are putting forward. It is often helpful or important if not necessary for the Disagreeable Thesis to be included as a counterargument.

As a cross-referencing tool: One of the easily overlooked advantages of using a secondary source is the way that a single article can guide you in finding other useful sources. As we move into the discussion of citations, it will be clear that systems of citation are designed for a reader (in this case, you) to find additional resources that the author employed. As such, an author's works-cited page, bibliography, and footnote/endnote system provide a list of sources that you might want to check out for your own purposes.

Citation

The French-American historian Jacques Barzun called the footnote a "badge of candor."[4] But why exactly? And what is the difference between a footnote, an endnote, and an in-text citation? Let us explain.

When you've read academic works, you've probably noticed two kinds of indicators that you don't see in any other kind of writing. The first appears as small numbers, called superscripts, at the end of some sentences. These point to additional information about the sentences. If this additional information is at the bottom of the page, it's called a footnote. If it's at the end of the chapter or book, it's called an endnote. Some of these notes contain carefully formatted lines that explain where the author got the sentence's idea, or in the case of a quotation, where the quote came from. In either case, these are called citations. The other kind of indicator appears in parentheses right after a sentence. Inside the parentheses is a number, or maybe a name and a year. These are called in-text citations. Citations are a commonly agreed-upon way to direct readers to the research sources you use. They are evidence of and an introduction

---

4. Jacques Barzun, *From Dawn to Decadence: 500 Years of Western Cultural Life* (New York: HarperCollins, 2000), 46.

to an ongoing intellectual conversation. They provide all the information needed to help a reader understand where you found your evidence, and how they can find it, too. So, honesty is at the heart of citations: the willingness to be truthful and trustworthy about where you have found your ideas and the words that express them.

Styles of Citation

Citation styles, sometimes called documentation styles, refer to the choices made about *how* to document sources. If you wanted, you could invent a citation style all on your own, name it after yourself (quite narcissistically), and then promote it on your blog, vlog, TikTok, or local library. We wish the best to you and your unique citation style, if you should go that route, but there's a problem: most people don't go that route. Most people rely on what most others use, for various and often good reasons.

In the case of academic citation styles, most people rely on those styles developed and maintained by academic organizations. These organizations curate choices made by professional scholars in relation to documenting sources. Consider the MLA style. MLA is the style of the Modern Language Association, an association founded in 1883 and with a current membership of over 23,000 across 145 countries. The MLA is the premier association in the United States for scholars and teachers of English and foreign languages, so it is natural that their citation style would be the go-to style for scholars and teachers of English and foreign languages, not to mention their students. The MLA style is the fruit of so many laborers in language departments across the United States.

The same is true of the APA style, which is the fruit of the American Psychological Association, "the leading scientific and professional organization representing psychology in the United States, with more than 157,000 researchers, educators, clinicians, consultants, and students as its members."[5] When writing a research paper in psychology (in the United States), it is best practice to use the APA style of citation. Physicists, chemists, biologists, and the like are also drawn to the APA style's scientific flavor, so use it frequently.

In addition to the MLA and APA styles, there is the "*Chicago* style," which is slightly unlike the other two, since it is not the product of a large academic association, but of a single university press: the University of Chicago Press. Chicago style began life in 1906 in the *Manual of Style: Being a compilation of the typographical rules in force at the University of Chicago Press, to which are appended specimens of type in use*, but it is now called, thankfully, *The Chicago Manual of Style*. We leave it up to you to figure out why this style guide from this particular university press became so famous, rivaling as it does the collective labors of the MLA and APA. The success of *The Chicago Manual of Style* might give you some hope for your own manual of style. You don't need to be a massive academic association to make your citation preferences the law of the land; you can also be a humble university press founded in 1890. Good luck to you.

Until then, all you have are the mixed joys of conformity.

So, let's get into some of the dirty details for each citation style, starting with MLA. But first, a warning: We're giving you the skeleton, not the muscles and organs, of these styles. We cannot cram three books (*The Publication Manual of the American Psychological Association*, *MLA Handbook*, and *The Chicago Manual of Style*) into one subsection. Nor would you want us to. For brevity and simplicity, we chose to focus

---

5. "About APA," American Psychological Association, last updated January 2022, https:///www.apa.org/about.

on the fundamentals, on the moves that will get you through 70 percent of your documentation troubles.

MLA STYLE

"Why is there so much bullshit?" (Frankfurt 62).

What we've provided above is a quotation from the book *On Bullshit* by the American philosopher Harry G. Frankfurt (one of our favorites). You'll notice that parenthetical bit that follows the quote; that is called an *in-text citation*, since it appears in the text itself (next to the text). In-text citations are short and sweet.

(Author's last name page number[s] where quote appears)

Short and sweet, yes, though MLA requires that this citation be expanded later in a list of "Works Cited," so savor your short in-text citations while you can. Our in-text citations can get even shorter:

As the American philosopher Harry G. Frankfurt asks, "Why is there so much bullshit?" (62).

Since we named the author of the quotation in our text, MLA allows us to omit the author's name from the in-text citation. Take note that, even if we don't quote Frankfurt, we still need an in-text citation if we reference him or otherwise use his work.

The vulgar slang "bullshit" can be a term of art in philosophy (Frankfurt).

In that example, we reference, and therefore cite, the entirety of Frankfurt's *On Bullshit*, not a specific page, so we need only the author's name. That is, until we flesh out the rest of the citation in the MLA's required "Works Cited" page, which we turn to now.

Our Frankfurt example is simple enough to cite in our Works Cited page:

Frankfurt, Harry G. *On Bullshit*. Princeton University Press, 2005.

It is simple, since this is a work by one author, so follows the MLA formula below:

Author's last name, first name. *Title*. Publisher, date of publication.

For a work by two authors, the MLA formula is this:

1st author's last name, first name, and 2nd author's first and last names. *Title*. Publisher, date of publication.

Here is a two-author example from our shelves:

Gutman, Amy, and Dennis Thompson. *The Spirit of Compromise: Why Governing Demands It and Campaigning Undermines It*. Princeton University Press, 2012.

For a work by three or more authors, we get the famous "et al.," which is an abbreviation of a Latin phrase that means "and others." Et al. is a space-and-time-saving device, though let's observe a moment of silence for those nonprimary authors whose names are lost in the convenience of et al.

1st author's last name, first name, et al. *Title*. Publisher, date of publication.

Here is another example from our shelves:

Newberg, Andrew, et al. *Why God Won't Go Away: Brain Science and the Biology of Belief*. Ballantine Books, 2001.

Let's use our three examples now to build a Works Cited page:

WORKS CITED

Frankfurt, Harry G. *On Bullshit*. Princeton University Press, 2005.

Gutman, Amy, and Dennis Thompson. *The Spirit of Compromise: Why Governing Demands It and Campaigning Undermines It*. Princeton University Press, 2012.

Newberg, Andrew, et al. *Why God Won't Go Away: Brain Science and the Biology of Belief*. Ballantine Books, 2001.

Note a few things about our Works Cited page. First, it is alphabetized, A–Z, using the last names of the authors. Second, it is double-spaced. Third, when the citation takes up more than one line, for example, our "Gutman, Amy" citation, we used a hanging indent (i.e., everything *but* the first line is indented); hanging indents help the eye differentiate citations. Finally, it is titled "Works Cited" and the title is centered. Clean and crisp, don't you think?

APA STYLE

APA and MLA are near relatives, but with some key dissimilarities. Like MLA, APA style requires in-text citations, but APA in-text citations are slightly more elaborate.

> "Why is there so much bullshit?" (Frankfurt, 2005, p. 62).

First, take note of the punctuation marks. MLA, with some exceptions, does not require these marks for in-text citations, but APA, for better or worse, does. It also requires that little "p." to signal that "p. 62" refers to page 62.

APA requires a year for in-text citations, which makes sense for a style geared toward scientific research, where lots of information becomes outdated quickly. The difference between "Phlogiston theory is well evidenced" (Becher, *1669*, p. 4) and "Phlogiston theory is well evidenced" (Becher, *2023*, p. 4) can say a lot to a scientific reader. In the 1669 case, the quote is likely of historical interest; in the 2023 case, the quote speaks to the current relevance of phlogiston theory (an *outdated* scientific theory).

In fact, years are so important in APA that they cannot always wait for the end of the sentence. If you mention the author in your sentence, you must immediately follow the author's name with a year.

As the American philosopher Harry G. Frankfurt (2005) asked, "Why is there so much bullshit?" (p. 62).

We can tell, at a glance, whether this Frankfurt individual is cutting-edge or stone-age.

Like MLA, in-text citations for APA use the space-and-time-saving "et al." for works by three or more authors.

Newberg et al. (2001) concluded that "mystical union and sexual bliss, therefore, use similar neural pathways" (p. 125).

Finally, like its MLA cousin, APA style requires a final list of everything you cited in your work. In the language of APA, this list is titled "References." Do not title your APA list of cited works "Works Cited." That would be like ordering a "large" cappuccino from Starbucks—the proper Starbucks term for large is "Venti."

Let's make a sample "References" page, starting with the required title, centered and bolded.

REFERENCES

Frankfurt, H. G. (2005). *On Bullshit*. Princeton University Press.

Newberg, A., D'Aquili, E., & Rause, V. (2001). *Why God Won't Go Away: Brain Science and the Biology of Belief*. Ballantine Books.

Does this feel a little like déjà vu? It looks like the MLA "Works Cited" page. Last names come first. Names are listed in alphabetical order. There is that hanging indent again. The lines are double-spaced. Feels familiar. But let's cover the differences. First, the first names are initialized; MLA's "Frankfurt, Harry G." becomes the APA's "Frankfurt, H. G." Secondly, APA uses the ampersand, "&," rather than "and" in a list of multiple authors. Finally, per the APA's date-obsessed style, the date comes right away, right after the name. APA style is like a person who checks their watch every ten minutes.

In good news, the APA honors those authors who are otherwise lost in the MLA's "et al." by requiring that all authors (or rather, all their last names and first initials) should be listed, unless you have more than twenty names—then some sacrifices will have to be made.

There is one other APA-specific element that our example references did not have: DOI. "DOI" means "digital object identifier." DOI is a unique number, similar in spirit to the URL you use to find a website, which helps us locate a source with little trouble. If your source has a DOI (and many sources do not), then you must include it in your citation on the References page, right at the end of your citation.

Here is an example citation with DOI, pulled from our trusty shelves:

Landgrebe, J., & Smith, B. (2022). *Why Machines Will Never Rule the World: Artificial Intelligence without Fear*. Routledge. DOI:10.4324/9781003310105.

It is not the loveliest thing to look at, but the DOI is part of the APA gift bag. When it comes to APA style, just remember the two D's: Dates and DOIs. If you see lots of parenthetical dates (years) in a text, and lots of DOIs in the references section, you're dealing with APA.

CHICAGO STYLE

Now clear your mind of MLA and APA. Our third and final style of citation, *Chicago* style, dances to the beat of a different drummer, a jazz drummer. While *Chicago* style does have a format for in-text citations, its "author-date" system, it allows writers to use an alternative "notes and bibliography" system. For some readers, in-text citations are just plain obtrusive; for these readers, moving citations out of the text, either down into a footnote or far, far away into an endnote, is the way to go. The notes-and-bibliography system keeps the reading experience smooth and flowing. See for yourself.[6] That tiny, unobtrusive, floating number at the end of the previous sentence is called a *superscript*, and it tells readers that a citation is afoot. That superscript points to a citation, so you don't have to insert the citation in the text. It points to a footnote, which sits at the "foot" of the page where the superscript occurs, or it points to an endnote, which comes toward the end of the whole work.

In this book, we use footnotes, as you've likely noticed. We've used them to cite our sources. In other words, this book uses the notes-and-bibliography system of *Chicago*

---

6. This is called a footnote, since it sits here at the "foot" of the page.

style So, consider this whole book an object lesson in *Chicago* style.

Here are some basic points to keep in mind about these notes. First, superscripted numbers should be ordered starting from 1, then on to 2, 3, 4, and so on, in the usual natural number sequence. In the form of footnotes, a citation must be at the bottom of a page and beneath a line (see footnote formatting below), to indicate "THESE ARE FOOT-NOTES!" Now, most word-processing software does the footnote/endnote formatting for us. Microsoft Word, the software we used to compose this book, has a special "Insert Footnote" and "Insert Endnote" button in its "References" menu, which makes the process easier than falling down a slide while sleeping. Other programs, such as Google Docs and Apple Pages, have similar make-it-painless buttons, so look out for them.

In any event, here is an example of how *Chicago* style citations work:

> Philosophers love to find both distinctions and similarities between things. In the class of similarities, take for instance one found by the American philosopher Harry G. Frankfurt: "There are similarities between hot air and excrement, incidentally, which make *hot air* seem an especially suitable equivalent for *bullshit*."[7]

If you've not yet looked down the page at the footnote # [7] for the citation, then please do so now; then come back here when you've finished. Welcome back. So, as you can see,

---

7. Harry G. Frankfurt, *On Bullshit* (Princeton, NJ: Princeton University Press, 2005), 43.

the structure of a note citation for *Chicago* style is simple enough:

Author's first name last name, *Title* (Place of publication:

Publisher, year of publication), page number.

Given that formula, our Frankfurt citation is formatted as such:

Harry G. Frankfurt, *On Bullshit* (Princeton, NJ: Princeton

University Press, 2005), 43.

Sometimes the "place of publication" can be confusing. Not because you can't find it (it is usually in the book's copyright page, in the first few pages of the book), but because the book may list several locations.

Fancy Book

by

Fancy Author

Famous Publisher

London, Paris, New York, Oxford, Cambridge,

Milan, Dubai, Xanadu

This is a rare problem, thankfully; most places of publication are clearly identifiable. However, if the place of publication isn't so clear, due to too many options, we recommend either picking the first from the list or picking the location closest to you geographically. Both suggestions have been made over the years by citation gurus. The important point is to get as many citation details as clear and consistent as you can, so that your readers can discern the sources you're using.

Finally, *Chicago* style, like MLA and APA, requires a big list of citations at the end of the work. *Chicago Manual of*

Style users call their citation list neither "Works Cited" nor "References," but the bubbly sounding "Bibliography." The citation format for the *Chicago* Bibliography is not radically unlike the reference lists of MLA and APA, but it is different, so here is the *Chicago* formula:

Author's last name, first name. *Title*. Place of publication: Publisher, year of publication.

Plugging in our Frankfurt book and one other book from above, we get our two-entry bibliography:

BIBLIOGRAPHY

Frankfurt, Harry G. *On Bullshit*. Princeton, NJ: Princeton University Press, 2005.

Landgrebe, Jobst, and Barry Smith. *Why Machines Will Never Rule the World: Artificial Intelligence without Fear*. New York: Routledge, 2022. https://doi.org/10.4324/978 1003310105.

Yes, even *Chicago* style would like you to add the DOI, if you have it. Our apologies.

FINAL ADVICE

MLA, APA, and *Chicago* style are the top three citation styles. Professors use them. Publishers use them. So, it helps to be familiar with them, and it helps even more to know how to find the places that will help you get familiar with them (e.g., Purdue Online Writing Lab). Our skeletal version here needs more; it needs a heart. How do you cite a multivolume work? How do you cite a translated work? How do you cite a newspaper, a blog entry, an online video, a social media post? Your journey into citations has only just begun.

Perhaps one of the most frustrating aspects of citation, the thing that may demoralize most people, is the seemingly perpetual updating of the various styles. Which edition of the *Chicago Manual of Style* is the most recent? The seventeenth edition? You could joke, with a note of exasperation in your delivery, that your smartphone's software updates are less frequent than these citation style updates. Imagine if the civic rules on how we wrote physical addresses were updated every two or three years. "Write your address clearly, but in the 8th version of 'MAIL' style." Would mail ever get to your friends and family?

The bitter truth is that *that* is life. Life evolves. The associations that oversee these citation standards are, thankfully, responsive to changes in the real world. We might wish that the speed of change were slower, here and elsewhere in our lives, but if we worked in these associations, we'd probably make the same decisions and recommend the same updates. The proliferation of different and even finer details may sometimes overwhelm you, but just know, most of us are slightly bugged by the carefully designed precision of these style guides.

Our final tip is simply this: get help. Get all the help you need. Don't hesitate to get help. Get the help of a librarian (online, in-person, over the phone, via pigeon, and so on). Join an online group that deals with citations, or better yet, a group that deals with citation anxiety. Employ the services of a professional copyeditor, if feasible. Use the best citation software (aka "reference management software") you can find (e.g., Zotero, Mendeley, or EndNote). Finally, buy the latest citation style guides, if your budget allows, or borrow them from the library, from friends, from wherever. Life can be hard, and "proper" citations are a small but sharp part of what makes life hard, but there are ways to make them bittersweet, and you must find them, but not necessarily by yourself. So, get help.

DO NOT PLAGIARIZE

If one of the primary objectives of writing is "making your mark," plagiarism, or the act of passing off another person's ideas and words as your own, short-circuits the whole endeavor. It is an act of deceiving your audience, but also of cheating yourself out of the opportunity to express your innermost thoughts and insights. Sure, you might not care about this opportunity at three in the morning, the day before an assignment, but you will when you wake up and compose yourself in the coming days. And you will feel guilty and always be slightly afraid of being caught— because you should be. "The fear of the Lord is true wisdom; to forsake evil is real understanding."[8] So reports the Book of Job, which is a good place to start our section on plagiarism, since fear, evil, and punishment are the usual themes of most discussions on plagiarism.

The key thing to keep in mind is this: if you plagiarize, you have cheated your audience and yourself. And if you plagiarize, *plagiarism software* will eventually catch you. It will. This is the twenty-first century, so forget about slipping a little plagiarism under the radar: the radar has become super-intelligent! To twist some words from the biblical Book of Job, "Fear of the radar is true wisdom." Honestly, our plagiarism software flags plagiarism *every term* in the work of at least two students. It is not the end of the world when you're caught plagiarizing (the radar is not weaponized yet), but for most of us, it doesn't feel good to be a plagiarist. Being a plagiarist means pretending to think when, in fact, you've done no such thing. It is, truly, pretentious.

The title of this book is *Thinking through Writing*. We take that title seriously. The sweetest fruit of writing is the

---

8. Job 28:28, New Living Translation.

growth of one's thought-life. When thoughts are "in our head," they are more cloudy, shadowy intuitions than what they become through writing—concrete, well-ordered, and intelligible realities. This is why shortcuts such as plagiarism and AI-generated writing (e.g., ChatGPT and other large language models) are only shortcuts in a superficial sense. Yes, they may help you pass a class, if you're good enough at counterfeiting, but these shortcuts do not take you to a healthy destination overall. These shortcuts keep you immature. Imagine if all your assignments, quizzes, exams, and projects, starting from first grade all the way to college graduation, were automatically and undetectably done for you by a powerful AI-assistant. What kind of intellect would you enjoy after all those years of letting AI do the hard work? Your thought-life would be undeveloped, likely just a dull mirror of the thoughts of others. Your arguments would be secondhand and hollow, your commentary a mass of undigested platitudes, and your understanding of the wide world a narrow caricature. Do yourself a favor and do the hard work to become a more thoughtful version of yourself.

How Does Plagiarism Happen?

So, how does plagiarism happen?

We are going to tell you, but you probably already know. When we tell you, it will sound like we are giving you a precise instruction manual on how to plagiarize, but—really—we are outlining a process that you should assiduously avoid. Think of it this way: the FBI's manual for preventing and catching money laundering can also be used as an instruction manual for money laundering. But if you use the manual for devious ends, you'll surely be caught.

The most common oopsie in plagiarism is *patchwriting*. In patchwriting, the offender pastes a chunk of someone else's text into what we call a "hot document" ("hot" as in "involving stolen goods"). To make the hot document less hot, the offender "cools" it down with a splash of synonyms, deletions, reorderings, and some original writing now and again to feel as though they did their fair share of the work. The offender, bless their heart, seems to assume that the plagiarism experts, linguists, and software engineers who design and update all of this state-of-the-art antiplagiarism software simply don't know the subtleties of patchwriting. The offender knows the subtleties, but not the entire industry of plagiarism experts.

Let's commit the crime together, as an object lesson. Let's rip off a few sentences from John's book *Hiking with Nietzsche*, including quoted material that he includes.

> In 1894, while Nietzsche rocked in the corner of an insane asylum, Salomé wrote his first biography, arguing that his tragic end was the only one that could have taken place. She insists that "we must direct our attention to the human being and not the theorist in order to find our way in Nietzsche's works. In that sense, our contemplation will not gain a new theoretical world picture but the picture of the human soul in all its greatness and sickliness."[9]

The first step in ripping off John is to *roget* his work (recall rogeting from earlier in this chapter). Our synonyms are italicized in the paragraph:

> In 1894, while Nietzsche *swayed* in the *nook* of a *mental institution*, Salomé wrote his first biography, *contending* that his *dreadful demise* was the

---

9. John Kaag, *Hiking with Nietzsche: On Becoming Who You Are* (New York: Farrar, Straus and Giroux, 2018), 97.

only one that could have *occurred*. She *asserts* that "we must direct our attention to the human being and not the theorist in order to find our way in Nietzsche's works. In that sense, our contemplation will not gain a new theoretical world picture but the picture of the human soul in all its greatness and sickliness."

Now that we've sprinkled some questionable synonyms into John's work, let's do a little rearranging, to make it less obvious to the casual reader that we're plagiarizing.

Salomé wrote Nietzsche's first biography in 1894, while Nietzsche *swayed* in the *nook* of a *mental institution*. She *contends* that Nietzsche's *dreadful demise* was the only one that could have *occurred*. She *asserts* that "we must direct our attention to the human being and not the theorist in order to find our way in Nietzsche's works. In that sense, our contemplation will not gain a new theoretical world picture but the picture of the human soul in all its greatness and sickliness."

Finally, let's be exceedingly courteous and add a thought or two of our own to this piece that we've pilfered from John. Our additions are put in bold:

Salomé wrote Nietzsche's first biography in 1894, while Nietzsche *swayed* in the *nook* of a *mental institution*, **like a broken pendulum.** She *contends*, **strangely enough,** that Nietzsche's *dreadful demise* was the only one that could have *occurred*. **Why?** She *asserts* that "we must direct our attention to the human being and not the theorist in order to find our way in Nietzsche's works. In that sense, our contemplation will not gain a new theoretical world picture but the picture of the human soul in all its greatness and sickliness." **Perhaps she was sickly too.**

Done! We have successfully plagiarized from John. It won't fool the plagiarism software, but fingers-crossed, no one will ever, ever, ever check. Now all we have to do is pretend for the rest of our lives that we wrote this paragraph from scratch.

Hopefully you've noticed that plagiarism is not exclusively about words, but ideas and structure too. In our example, John's structure frames the quotation chosen. We've pilfered not only John's analysis, but also the exact chunk of quotation he analyzes. John built the window frame, selected its location in the wall, installed the frame and the glass panes, then added curtains as a finishing touch. We just changed the curtains.

Naturally, not all plagiarism is so deliberate. Some plagiarism is a result of disorganization. In the course of research, you might hastily jot down a sentence you found in an old magazine, but forget, in your haste, to put quotation marks around it or put anything that identifies that this is *not* your sentence. Later, you find this jotting among so many other jottings and just assume that you're the Clever Christopher who wrote it. You don't remember writing it, but your cleverness is superior to your memory, so yes, of course, it is likely yours. So, you plagiarize, but with a clean conscience. It happens.

Sometimes you plagiarize because you don't think that the material itself qualifies as *able to be plagiarized*. Does a song lyric count? A personal text from a friend? What about that skywriting you saw the other day? You've heard that content "in the public domain" can be used without violating any copyright, so do you need to cite and cite public domain content? And what about recipes, idioms, or mathematical formulas? Is there an ultimate and unchanging directory of what sorts of things need acknowledgment and what sorts of things don't? Perhaps Google knows!

We have some suggestions.

How to Avoid Plagiarism

There is a simple, though not easy rule for acknowledgments: *safety first*. Whenever you're incorporating anything into your writing that did not spring directly from your own spontaneous acts of writing, acknowledge it. To put that advice into rhyme:

If you didn't write it, cite it.

If you stay faithful to that rhyming rule, your chances of plagiarizing plummet to a *virtual* zero. Citation, which we explored in the previous section, is the best lawyer you can get for defending yourself against charges of plagiarism.

Yet even a citation, like a lawyer, has its limits. Your work needs to be clearly differentiated from the work of others. For example, suppose you take our plagiarized paragraph from above, the one about Nietzsche, and simply slap a citation on its tail end: John Kaag, *Hiking with Nietzsche: On Becoming Who You Are* (New York: Farrar, Straus and Giroux, 2018), 97. Presto chango, plagiarism be gone! Except not. It is dishonest to simply copy-and-paste the original work of others, fail to put quote marks where appropriate (pause and repeat this last point to yourself), scramble the material up a little, and then pass it off as yours. To avoid plagiarism, you need to make it crystal clear when you use the words, structures, or ideas of others. A randomly placed citation, with no sense of its scope, with no sense of which bits and scraps belong to which writer, fails to count as making things crystal clear. That is smoggy. Don't be a smoggy writer.

Now in the case of disorganization, where you use the work of others unintentionally due to poor note-taking, the cure is better note-taking. Every time (repeat: every time) you jot down a phrase or line from another work, put it in quotes and indicate, in whatever way you need, that it is *not* your work. Ideally, you will also add information about the source itself, but as long as your notes show clearly that you did not write that content, there should be no *unintentional* plagiarism later on.

Finally, what content *requires* acknowledgment? Unfortunately, we don't have a prepared list for you (it would be too long), but if we were forced to make a list for you now, it would be this: *all of it*. What harm could it do to anyone to become a fanatic about sources? You can even source sky-writing: The skywriting read, "Will You Marry Me, Donna?" (Skywriting seen by the author in Portland, Oregon, August 8, 2023, around 4:00 p.m. local time). Whether or not someone will require you to source skywriting depends on that someone, but no one can fault you for plagiarism, or even intent to plagiarize, if you've quoted and cited so fanatically that historians three thousand years from now can use your work to reconstruct our civilization. That's hyperbole, but hopefully helpful hyperbole.

Marginal Cases of Plagiarism

OK, yes, there remain a few hard cases, or marginal cases, where acknowledgment just seems unnecessary and, worse, excessive. Let's consider two: (1) self-plagiarism and (2) short or generic sentences.

SELF-PLAGIARISM

"Self-plagiarism" may sound like a contradiction in terms. How can you plagiarize yourself!?[10] What about that nice

---

10. FYI, the punctuation mark "!?" (aka "?!" or "!?!" or even "?!?") is called an *interrobang*. Save that gem for trivia night.

rhyming rule above? Now, we learn, even if we did write it, we must still cite it? What isn't plagiarism? We hear you ask: "Do I have to cite my secret diary if I borrow a line from it?"

With some exceptions, such as that secret diary, we do recommend you cite and quote your previously completed or published work. Don't cheat your past self. Acknowledge their labor. Consider this an opportunity to recommend to readers your other accomplishments. Sometimes it is a small thrill, a very small thrill, to see your name listed in a Bibliography or Works Cited page; it is a confidence boost for some of us.

SHORT OR GENERIC SENTENCES

Honestly now, how many ways can you paraphrase "He died in 1984"? Let's try:

> *The man perished in the eighty-fourth year of the 1900s.*
> *Sixteen years before the second millennium, he died.*
> *His year of death: 1984.*
> *He passed away in the mid-eighties.*
> *His life ended the year that Indira Gandhi was assassinated.*

None of those paraphrases are as crisp and clean as the original. But what if all we need for our essay is that mortality fact from our hypothetical source; must we, ethically or legally, quote and cite our source for "He died in 1984"? Or, are we doomed to stilted paraphrases of short and generic sentences?

The irksome answer is this: it depends.

Sometimes a fact, claim, or phrase is "unique enough" to merit acknowledgment of the source, and sometimes a fact, claim, or phrase is "common enough" to be part of that mass of "universal" content that we're allowed to use without acknowledgment. We quote those qualifiers to indicate their fuzziness and slipperiness. What is "unique enough"? What is "universal" content? Those are tough questions even for us to answer.

Friedrich Nietzsche died in August of 1900. We know that because we read it long ago, then read it again and again in various trustworthy sources. At this point, we feel comfortable writing that "Nietzsche died in August of 1900" without acknowledging all that reading we did to come to know that fact. Are we plagiarizing all of those sources? No. Why? Because the fact seems to us generic enough, or belonging to no one in particular. We couldn't even paraphrase an original version of this statement, since we make this claim without reference to an original version of this statement; we've simply absorbed a truth about Nietzsche. Do you remember the first time someone told you the earth revolves around the sun? How about all the other times you heard that statement reaffirmed?

Some statements just don't need acknowledgment, but there's no scientific procedure to show us which ones. Writing and thinking remain an art, for this reason and others. All we can hope for is that you practice your art in good faith.

EXERCISES

1. Describe the difference between a primary and secondary source; then give a real example of a primary and secondary source for one writing topic you are working on or have worked on. For example,

   A primary source is [—], whereas a secondary source is [—]. For example, if I write about Henry David Thoreau's time at Walden Pond, *Walden* by Thoreau would be a primary source for me, while Robert D. Richardson's biography of Thoreau, *Henry David Thoreau: A Life of the Mind*, would be a secondary source for me.

2. Use the following data from a single-author book to make a *Chicago* style entry for a bibliography.

Year of publication: 2014
Place of publication: Tucson, Arizona
Publisher: University of Arizona Press
Author: Michelle M. Jacob
Title of book: *Yakama Rising: Indigenous Cultural Revitalization, Activism, and Healing*

Now, use that same data, adding the data point of page number 18, and make a *Chicago* style note. Finally, find a book on your shelf and create a *Chicago* style bibliography entry and note based on that source.

3. Write a short paragraph describing what it feels like when someone takes credit for work that you did that they did not. If you felt wronged, what do those feelings of being wronged tell you? Or, if you've ever taken credit for work that someone else did, write about why you did that and how the other person might feel if they knew.

Chapter 7

THINKING THROUGH TECHNIQUE

EDITING AND REVISION

"Of all that is written," Friedrich Nietzsche tells his reader, "I love only what a person hath written with his blood. Write with blood, and thou wilt find that blood is spirit."[1] The point of writing, if we understand Nietzsche correctly, is to cut to the bone: to put your real no-bullshit self on paper. But it is also to be willing to endure some hardship—at least a little—and this involves painful writerly revision. At some point, all authors cherish once pristine, now-rumpled pages as the most accurate renderings of them-selves. In the process of writing and revising, however, one usually has to sacrifice the self-knowledge that one thinks he or she already has (that the current draft is surely the best that it can be), to give up some version of your past self for a better and more accurate portrait.

Editing is not a matter of "murdering your darlings" (the parts of your writing that you love, but that don't fit), but sacrificing them so something else more aligned can take their place. The traces of mistakes and failed attempts haunt many books, but the best authors, like Nietzsche, in-corporate them into the vibrancy of a literary corpus. "I have often asked myself," Nietzsche writes, "whether I am not more deeply indebted to the most difficult years of my

---

1. Friedrich Nietzsche, *Thus Spake Zarathustra*, trans. Thomas Common (New York: Heritage Press, 1967), 35.

life than any of the others."[2] An author is indebted, and so obligated, to embrace and amend failures in the course of writing, the mistakes that allow it to become what it is.

How to Draft an Essay

The best-selling author Anne Lamott once said that the key to writing anything well is to start with a "shitty first draft."[3] Expecting your first draft to be "shitty" has a number of virtues: it relieves you of the undue pressure of being perfect; it encourages you to write quickly without agonizing about details; and it provides a rough sketch that can be refined and fleshed out in the course of revision. Assume that you will write two or three drafts before you write a final one. Writing is largely a process of revision. "Writing is rewriting," goes an old saying.

Start your first draft by writing a coherent introduction in one sitting, making sure that its anatomy or organization includes at least the motivation, thesis, and methodology for the paper. You can walk away from your notepad or computer for a little while after the introduction is finished, but within an hour you need to be back at your draft. Now, take a look at the outline or notes that you have taken in the course of research, organize your thoughts, and begin writing your supporting body paragraphs.

Write the body of your essay also in one sitting (a rough rule of thumb is two hours for a two-thousand-word paper). If you have to get up and interrupt yourself, make sure you leave "breadcrumbs," a series of notes that tell you

---

2. Friedrich Nietzsche, *The Complete Works of Friedrich Nietzsche*, vol. 9, *Nietzsche Contra Wagner* (Stanford: Stanford University Press, 2021), 405.

3. Anne Lamott, *Bird by Bird: Some Instructions on Writing and Life* (New York: Anchor Books, 1995), 21–27.

what you still need to do in the course of your draft. On this first draft, don't worry about the nitty gritty details — citations, dates, spelling — just get the ideas out as fast as possible. You will encounter unexpected turns in the course of your argument. Go with them long enough to see where they lead. Always let them lead back to your thesis, and if they veer too far afield, cut them off and take a new route. Of course, you can revise your thesis, and that will adjust the argument and the discussion that you want to present, but don't revise forever. Nothing ventured nothing gained. If a paragraph is not working for you, don't dwell on it too long. Start the next one and try to stick with it. Remember: "shitty" is the key word in "shitty first draft." When you get to the end of the first draft, that is a good time to reassess.

RESPONSE AND REVISION

Once you finish the draft, it's time to think through your own writing with a critical eye. You may already see problems. If you don't, look again, or hand the first draft to a peer-reader. Editing your own writing is largely a matter of figuring out how to use "scissors" and "glue." You can cut sections of an essay apart or cut them out entirely. Cutting sentences and paragraphs may allow you to make a point more forcefully and directly. You can also reorder sections, gluing them back together in a new sequence. Ask yourself whether reordering paragraphs might allow your reader to move between ideas in a more fluid or compelling way. And you can add new material to strengthen the argument that you are making. Details, sources, and examples that were missing in the first draft need to be integrated in the appropriate paragraphs. A good editor will make four distinct "passes" on a draft, a first focusing on content, a second on sentence structure, a third on the cohesion of paragraphs, and a fourth evaluating the use of language.

CONTENT-LEVEL EDITING

1. First drafts, by virtue of their rough-and-ready nature, lack focus. Can you tighten or hone your thesis to make a clearer claim?

2. You might have forgotten to motivate the urgency or importance of your claim or provide the necessary context for a reader to understand your thesis.

3. Check each body paragraph: do you need to make additional distinctions, provide more evidence, or give more complex reasons to support your thesis? Are there other sources or texts that might supplement your argument?

4. Check for conceptual cohesion (do the ideas fit together?)

SENTENCE-LEVEL EDITING

1. Does every sentence sound coherent and clear?

2. Does every sentence exhibit proper punctuation?

3. Does each sentence employ a transition from previous sentences, linking ideas and keywords in a way that a reader can follow?

4. Do your sentences vary in length and construction? Variation is good.

5. Are all sentences written in the active voice?

6. Do you see the word "that" or the phrases "there is" and "it is"? These are telltale signs of wooden prose, prose that sounds unnatural, like a bad actor reading an equally bad script.

7. Do you see locutions like "needless to say" or "it goes without saying" or "and so on" or "and so forth"? These are unnecessary fillers.

8. Use your computer's spell-check and grammar-check (even a program like Grammarly), but never trust their findings blindly.

PARAGRAPH-LEVEL EDITING

1. Does each paragraph have an effective topic sentence that announces the issue at hand in the paragraph?
2. Does the paragraph gesture or look back to earlier points or premises, and gesture forward to future steps in your argument?
3. Is evidence well integrated in your text? Do you set the context for quotations or explain them in subsequent sentences?
4. Can your paragraph be split into multiple ones? Are there too many ideas being expressed in a single block of text?

AN EDITING SCHEDULE

Editing takes time—to think, to adapt, to think some more—which means that writers need to schedule an adequate period between the completion of their first draft and the due date. For any substantial piece of writing, we like to give ourselves approximately a week lead time for the process of editing. Sometimes we have to write for looming deadlines, and this time is compressed, but in any case, we divide our editing time into digestible short-term goals. Take a look at our normal editing schedule.

Day one: Read your essay forward (for content, making marks where needed).

Day two: Read your essay backward (for sentence and paragraph structure and word choice).

Day three: Make corrections (guided by the marks you made on days one and two).

Day four: Have someone else read it.

Day five: Make final touches.

Day six: Kiss it goodbye and celebrate.

Day seven: Rest.

CONCISION

What Is Concision?

We capped this subsection at five hundred words (and came in a little under), so consider this subsection a demonstration of concision. As such, we recommend you hone it further. Once you finish all three subsections on concision, make this subsection more concise. Distill it down to four hundred words (or two hundred!) without sacrificing meaning.

First, of course, let's help *you* help *us* by learning about concision.

Concision means using fewer words *for your purpose*. If you can convey the same meaning in ten words instead of thirteen, ask yourself: why those extra three words? A good editor will ask about those three extra words, so have a good reason, or clean up accordingly. You may occasionally need a sentence as lengthy as a paragraph, with dependent clauses, intricately nested, and that may be the most concise you can be to achieve your purpose, but do distrust your meandering sentences, especially in their first-draft form.

One serviceable test of concision is boredom. Does the sentence bore you? If so, it is likely *not* concise. Let's take an example of a sentence that bored us and revise it for concision.

> *Boring sentence*: "There is a good deal to explore in regard to boredom and subsequent chapters will address the many aspects of this common emotion gaining [its] place in the study of emotions as well as in [its] relation to learning, as boredom can interfere with school success and learning."[4]

---

4. Gayle L. Macklem, *Boredom in the Classroom: Addressing Student Motivation, Self-Regulation, and Engagement in Learning* (New York: Springer International Publishing, 2015), 10.

Revision: Boredom is fascinating, so in coming chapters we explore this common emotion and how it hooks into learning, success in school, and, increasingly, the study of emotions.

Our revision is not perfect, but it is, without sacrificing substance, *less* boring. We hope. Plus, forty-eight words boiled into twenty-seven leaves you less time to become bored.

Years ago, Jonathan was inspired by Harry Frankfurt's *On Bullshit* and Japanese shuriken, aka the "ninja star," to design a series of philosophy books appealing to time-poor philosophers, tiny-book collectors, and finish-a-book-a-day enthusiasts. Each book would be 3.5 inches wide and 5.5 inches tall, and capped at 100 pages. Each title would be six words or less; the shorter the better. Shuriken books would open with a summary, no longer than one page, so that the crux of the book may be speedily absorbed. Shuriken books (not *shrunken* books, but similar) would demand a merciless compression of ideas into their punchiest form. Directness and sharpness.

Jonathan's Shuriken series is yet to be made, unfortunately. Yet some of the central texts of philosophy are short and sweet: Thomas More's *Utopia*, René Descartes's *Meditations on First Philosophy*, John Stuart Mill's *Utilitarianism*. All three are wafer-thin volumes, yet monumental in impact. Harry Frankfurt's *On Bullshit*, while less monumental, is even thinner. In *On Bullshit*, Frankfurt cut the bullshit so efficiently that it required only sixty-seven pages to make his case travel around the world and sell more than a million copies.

On the Joys of Cutting

Cutting words and sentences can be more fun than writing them. For some editors, cutting out an author's excess may be more mouthwatering than cutting a birthday cake. An example of this devilish joy may help, so let's edit John Ruskin, the Victorian English polymath, who here preaches concision:

> Say all you have to say in the fewest possible words, or your reader will be sure to skip them; and in the plainest possible words or he will certainly misunderstand them.[5]

Wise counsel, indeed, but let's get out our surgical equipment and give Ruskin a taste of his own Victorian cure:

> Say all you have to say in the fewest ~~possible~~ words, or your reader will ~~be sure to~~ skip them; and in the plainest ~~possible~~ words or he will ~~certainly~~ misunderstand them.

In our cuts, did we lose anything essential? Notice that we removed "possible" in two places: after "fewest" and "plainest." "Fewest" and "plainest" express the superlative degree of "few" and "plain." Is it possible for there to be fewer than "fewest"? No. Is it possible to be plainer than the "plainest"? No. So, there is no clear difference between "fewest words" and "fewest possible words"; thus, if we wished to make cuts to Ruskin's words, we could cut here without killing the patient.

"Certainly" is safely removed too, since the clause "he will misunderstand them" leaves no wiggle room about his misunderstanding. It is not "he might," but the fateful "he will." His fate is certain, so spare the poor chap the unnecessary word "certainly." For the same reason, we can spare him "be sure to."

5. John Ruskin, *A Joy for Ever*, 2nd ed. (London: George Allen, 1895), 163.

Note how Ruskin's voice is lost a little by our cuts. Some emphasis is gone, for example, in the expressions "will be sure to" and "he will certainly." Keep in mind that cutting is a tool, not a commandment; sometimes voice or style should be prioritized over concision. A reader might skip a crisp and technically "perfect" sentence to get to sentences that, while imperfect or redundant, serve a separate aesthetic purpose. All effects on the reader should be considered. We might like Ruskin's faintly purplish Victorian prose, concision be damned.

Cutting, of course, is not the same as concision. Other techniques for concision exist, as we'll show next. Cutting is only the easiest option. We generally like to start with the easiest option. Why? Life is already difficult enough.

Grammatical Tips for Concise Writing
EIGHT TIPS FOR TRIMMING PROSE LIKE HEMINGWAY
IN A HOSTILE MOOD

1. Kill Pleonasms to Death!

A pleonasm is a redundancy. *He was killed to death. I was born at a young age.* Those are obvious pleonasms. In that Ruskin quote just discussed, we found two subtle pleonasms: "fewest possible words" and "plainest possible words." Pleonasms are more common than you may think. Consider RAS syndrome, or "Redundant Acronym Syndrome syndrome." Stricken with RAS syndrome, we write pleonasms such as ATM machine, SAT test, and PDF format.

The comedian George Carlin wrote, in our minds, the funniest pleonastic paragraphs in his collection *When Will Jesus Bring the Pork Chops?*

I needed a new beginning, so I decided to pay a social visit to a personal friend with whom I share the same mutual objectives and who is one of the most unique individuals I have ever personally met. The end result was an unexpected surprise. When I reiterated again to her the fact that I needed a fresh start, she said I was exactly right; and, as an added plus, she came up with a final solution that was absolutely perfect.

Based on her past experience, she felt we needed to join together in a common bond for a combined total of twenty-four hours a day, in order to find some new initiatives. What a novel innovation! And, as an extra bonus, she presented me with the free gift of a tuna fish. Right away I noticed an immediate positive improvement. And although my recovery is not totally complete, the sum total is I feel much better now knowing I am not uniquely alone.[6]

A "concise pleonasm" is like a "frugal gambler"—a term pulling in opposite directions. For concision's sake, cut all pleonasms.

2. Fold Prepositional Phrases into Adjectives.

Prepositional phrases can act as adjectives, and sometimes we can replace those prepositional phrases with a single adjective. Consider the adjectival prepositional phrases (each italicized) below:

My mansion *on the coast* burned down.

John's cabin *in the mountains* also burned down.

Let's concisify those.

My *coastal* mansion burned down.

John's *mountain* cabin also burned down.

6. George Carlin, *When Will Jesus Bring the Pork Chops?* (New York: Hyperion, 2004), 10–11.

3. Be Precise.

Precise words are key to concision. Consider this sixteen-word sentence: "You copied the writing of someone else and presented it as if it were your own!" With a precise word, we get the same meaning in a mere two words: "You plagiarized!"

> Before: I love the coldest season of the year.

> After: I love winter.

> Before: Rashid is an unmarried male.

> After: Rashid is a bachelor.

When choosing a precise word, be careful to avoid archaic and obscure ones (see tip 5 in this list). Precision, like concision, is not the be-all and end-all of good writing. Perhaps nothing is.

4. Filler, So to Speak, Must, If You Will, Be Cut, as They Say.

Filler is "noise-shaped air," as the character Dan Egan says in the HBO series *Veep*. Dan's metaphor refers to an early draft of a presidential speech, a genre famous for exhaling air at high temperatures. Yes, filler is that "hot air" you hear about. Or rather, it is hot *breath*. Most people dislike hot breath in their face, and we would bet that most people dislike it in their sentences too.

Filler is stuff you can lose and no one would miss it. Here are some usual offenders:

> There were
> As a matter of fact
> For all intents and purposes
> Basically
> By and large
> It appears

In terms of
The sort of thing that
In order to
Very

The list could drag on. Hot breath everywhere (hot *dragon* breath).

To avoid filler, we recommend the "Twitter edit." Twitter (now "X") once capped a single tweet at 280 characters (that includes spaces and punctuation marks). That constraint forces concision.[7] In a Twitter edit, you draft a tweet of a sentence or two or, better yet, three. Twitter's software counts down to your limit and highlights excess characters in an alarming red. You revise until you're out of the red. The end.

Let's Twitter-edit that last paragraph.

We suggest the "Twitter edit." Tweets were once capped at 280 characters, which forced concision. In Twitter edits, you draft a tweet of one to three sentences, the software counts down to your limit, highlighting excess characters in red, and you revise until you're out of the red.

Our original paragraph was not bursting with filler, we would argue, yet the Twitter edit shows how much more concise we still could be. Why weren't we more concise in the first place then? Did we violate our own rules? Or did we make that paragraph slightly wordy *knowing* that we would Twitter-edit it?[8]

---

7. Warning: We do not recommend Twitter as a style guide, where incorrect spellings and poor grammar run amok. The "Twitter Edit" is an assessment of concision and nothing more.

8. Answer: We didn't plan to Twitter-edit that paragraph, but we also didn't violate our own rules, as these are tips, not rules.

5. Keep It Simple, You Lexiphanes with Your Sesquipedalian Lucubrations!

This tip should be easy: don't abuse your thesaurus. Avoid those words labeled "archaic" or "obscure" in dictionaries. Why would you choose "peccaminous" over "sinful" or "cerumen" over "earwax"? Are you a doctor? Are you living in the baroque period? Are you a trivia master? Are you fearful of being a commoner like us with our simple words in easy-to-read sentences?

Concision calls for using fewer words *for your purpose*, and sometimes you need archaic or obscure words to achieve your purpose, but a dash of Tabasco does not mean dumping a full bottle of it into the chili. Don't overseason your sentences. To be frank, if you pile on the fancy synonyms, not only do you sacrifice concision, but you sound like a person with linguistic insecurities trying hard to sound intelligent. It is cringey to read such hot messes. More importantly, ten-dollar words tend to confuse your intended message. Please stop.

6. Activate the Active Voice.

When you find verbs such as "be," "been," "being," "is," "are," "were," "was" (forms of the auxiliary verb "be") followed by another verb ending with "-ed," "-en," "-n," "-d," "-t" (past participles), then you have found yourself *being* treat*ed* to the passive voice. You *are being* treat*ed* passively.

The passive voice is usually wordier than the active voice, so less friendly to concise writing.

> Passive voice: That miniature schnauzer *is being* tak*en* on a walk by that German shepherd.

> Active voice: That German shepherd is walking that miniature schnauzer.

> Passive voice: Rand and Nance *were* fir*ed* from the Cheesecake Factory.

Active voice: The Cheesecake Factory fired Rand and Nance.

Another signal of the passive voice is the mysterious presence of "it." "It," via the passive voice, becomes a dummy pronoun, meaning a pronoun that refers to nothing, but adds a grammatical subject.[9] Like a ventriloquist's dummy, a dummy pronoun doesn't talk, yet it moves its mouth.

Passive voice: It is the preference of readers to skip this grammar example.

Active voice: Readers prefer skipping this grammar example.

7. Combine Sentences.

"Two for the price of one!" shout the endless advertisements. Let's pretend those ads implore us to combine two sentences (or more) into one concise sentence. Let's combine the next two sentences:

Original: "In the World War, we used propaganda to make the boys accept conscription. They were made to feel ashamed if they didn't join the army."[10]

Combination: In the World War, we used propaganda to make the boys accept conscription and feel ashamed if they didn't join the army.

In that example, we added "and" and deleted "they were made to." Simple. Sometimes combining sentences is less simple. The next example requires more than deletion.

---

9. Note that the "it" in "it refers to nothing" is *not* a dummy pronoun, since it refers back to the subject of our discussion, the dummy pronoun "it." Not all cases of "it" are dummy pronouns.

10. Smedley D. Butler, *War Is a Racket* (Port Townsend, WA: Feral House, 2003), 35.

Original: "We are not drug addicts. We are not criminals. We are free men, and we will react to persecution the way free men have always reacted."[11]

Combination: We are neither drug addicts nor criminals, but free men who will react to persecution the way free men have always reacted.

We shaved off four words there. Was it worth it? If word count is paramount, yes. If we consider rhetorical power, we think concision here worsened the original. Again, concision is not about cutting words, but resisting wordiness. It is subservient to your other purposes, such as rhetorical forcefulness. Sometimes your purposes require short sentences: for emphasis, for varying the rhythm of paragraphs, for memorableness, and so on. These are the points in your essay where you could combine sentences, but shouldn't. So don't combine willy-nilly. Combine wisely.

8. If You Feel Unsure about Cutting It, Cut It.

This final tip is simple: cut when uncertain. If the writing feels "iffy," "not quite right," "awkward," or otherwise "bleh," cut it. If it doesn't sound good to you *now*, it is unlikely to sound good to you *later*. Sometimes silence is the perfect sentence. Favor cutting over keeping, but be careful to cut cleanly; cut to the chase, but don't cut *the chase*. The art of cutting elegantly takes practice, so we recommend starting as soon as possible, as we will now, by cutting to the end of this chapter.[12]

---

11. Arthur Kleps, testifying before the Special Senate Judiciary Subcommittee on Narcotics, May 25, 1966, as cited in Walter Houston Clark, *Chemical Ecstasy: Psychedelic Drugs and Religion* (New York: Sheed and Ward, 1969), 140.

12. We wish to confess: there is a nonzero chance you will find filler, pleonasms, and passive voice in this book. We are all hypocrites, but we can work toward *less* hypocrisy. If you find such hypocrisies in our book, please contact us with information regarding their whereabouts, and we will, as everyone must, revise, revise, revise.

A TIME AND PLACE FOR GRAMMAR

Thomas de Mahy, the Marquis de Favras, was executed in 1790 for conspiracy against the people of France. Though the case against him was weak, the partisan spirit of the French Revolution filled in the judicial blanks and doomed him to the gallows. Yet up there on the gallows, seconds from a neck-snapping fall through the floor, presented with his death warrant, the Marquis said wryly, "Vous avez fait, monsieur, trois fautes d'autographe" ("You have made, sir, three spelling mistakes").[13]

Syntax

Sometimes grammar is beside the point, as in the case of Marquis de Favras, but in the vast majority of cases, it is not. Here is the good news: you already know a whole lot about grammar. Speech is punctuated, naturally. Read this aloud:

> The breaths I take, like that one, indicate commas or, in this case, a period.
> The inflections in one's voice: a colon.
> Another—an em dash.
> Compound sentences, like this one, roll off the tongue naturally, and they enter our speech without us toiling over their construction.
> Now I can stop reading out loud.

Writing grammatically, however, is not at all natural. It takes practice, a little of which we want to give you here. In our experience, you can teach grammar in two ways. You can tell a student what not to do, or you can encourage a student to do the right thing, that is, to write simple

13. Wikipedia, s.v. "Thomas de Mahy de Favras," last modified October 25, 2023, https://fr.wikipedia.org/wiki/Thomas_de_Mahy_de_Favras.

sentences correctly with the help of syntax. Let's start with this second way. Syntax is a scary sounding word for a pretty simple concept.

Syntax is just the way that you order written words in order to construct well-formed sentences in any language. The basic unit of syntax is called a clause, which includes a subject and a predicate. Or more simply, a noun phrase plus a verb phrase. That is what a basic sentence is. A clause is independent when it has a subject, verb, and expresses a complete thought. Independent clauses are very basic units of expression; they don't have to say much to express a complete thought. Consider this phrase:

Rhonda and Troy

This phrase has only a subject: it's about Rhonda and Troy. But it says nothing about their relation or what they're doing. Now consider this:

Rhonda and Troy explore.

By adding this single word, which is a verb, the phrase becomes an independent clause, a sentence. Admittedly, it's not a fulfilling sentence. It doesn't tell us much about what they're exploring, or why, or what they feel about it. But insofar as it has a noun phrase and a verb phrase, it's expressing a complete thought. Thoughts can be incomplete in a second way, by having no subject phrase. Consider:

because it was tired

or

came home after work today

Both of these phrases express a relationship or action, but they remain incomplete. In this state, they're dependent clauses. What they lack is a sense of who is acting, who is tired, or who is coming home. Adding a noun, like

John came home after work today

or an independent clause like

The cat slept because it was tired

completes the thought and creates an independent clause. The key question to use in identifying an independent clause is "Are these words a sentence?" which is to say "Is this a complete thought?" Now, here's some more good news about grammar and independent clauses. There are only really four types of basic sentences.

SENTENCES WITH "BE" VERBS

Among English words, "be" is unusual. It's basic, present in many of the sentences we write or speak every day. It's also slippery, able to play many roles. One role it can play is to call out existence. A simple thought like

I am

or

Napoleon was

is a complete thought, so they're independent clauses and also sentences. These clauses can be significantly more developed, though they'll still work in the same way. Consider:

The French political and military leader who ascended to power and became Emperor in 1804 was.

One might imagine the latter sentence as an inelegant but correct answer to the question "Who was Napoleon"? But this isn't the only way the verb "be" can be used. For instance,

Tanya's cold (Tanya is cold).

is a sentence, too. This use of "be" is a little different than the first ones. In this case, it's connecting the first word, "Tanya," to the third, "cold." We can call this usage a "linking verb."

SENTENCES WITH LINKING VERBS

Clauses with linking verbs are always sentences. Linking verbs, sometimes called copulative verbs, are those that establish a relationship between a subject and an adjective. Adjectives are those words that name an attribute in order to modify a noun (person, place, or thing). In the earlier

Tanya is cold.

it is clear that "is" connects "cold" and "Tanya" by claiming that the former is true of the latter. This same kind of relationship holds in a sentence like

Kathleen looks beautiful.

or

Shinichi remains sad.

There's no action in either of these sentences; the verbs only signal the attachment of the adjectives to their subjects. Kathleen's state of being beautiful and Shinichi's sadness are asserted, and these are basic—but complete!—thoughts. For that reason, they're sentences.

The two remaining kinds of basic sentences are those where action happens. In the first case, the action will be carried out on an object. In the second, no object will be needed.

SENTENCES USING TRANSITIVE VERBS WITH DIRECT OBJECTS

Transitive verbs are those that point to a direct object on which a subject is acting. Take the phrase

Sam summons.

While this is an appropriate noun-verb pairing, it's clear something is missing: who or what's being summoned? To complete the thought and fill out the sentence, a further term or phrase, called an object, is added. For example:

Sam summons the waiter.

or

Sam summons the police.

or

Sam summons demons.

And so on. Many verbs we use every day—like "calls," "teaches," "drives"—function in just this same way, pointing to an object beyond themselves, but not all verbs do. This brings us to our last set of basic sentences, those with intransitive verbs.

SENTENCES WITH INTRANSITIVE VERBS

Intransitive verbs are those that do not point to an object. Consider the verb "laughs."

Sadie laughs.

Though we can ask how Sadie laughs—and use adverbs such as loudly or softly—the question "what does Sadie laugh?" makes no sense. Many verbs of bodily movement— such as "sleeps" and "snores," two enjoyable activities— are intransitive. *To easily determine whether you're working with a transitive or intransitive verb, just ask whether it points to something beyond itself to complete the thought.* If you have trouble remembering these, remember this: *the short sentence is your friend.* If you keep your sentences short, they will naturally fall into the above forms. Keep it simple. Brevity is the soul of wit. If simplicity is the baseline in your writing, it also gives you the chance, like the chance that we are right now, to juxtapose short sentences with much longer, more complex ones. Get it?

Let's now look together at a longer passage to get a sense of how independent and dependent clauses work together to build sentences and meaning. The following excerpt is from the introduction to Ta-Nehisi Coates's "The Case for Reparations" from the *Atlantic*, which outlines the history of African American oppression in the United States, using the Ross family as a case study:

> The losses mounted. As sharecroppers, the Ross family saw their wages treated as the landlord's slush fund. Landowners were supposed to split the profits from the cotton fields with sharecroppers. But bales would often disappear during the count, or the split might be altered on a whim. If cotton was selling for 50 cents a pound, the Ross family

might get 15 cents, or only five. One year Ross's mother promised to buy him a $7 suit for a summer program at their church. She ordered the suit by mail. But that year Ross's family was paid only five cents a pound for cotton. The mailman arrived with the suit. The Rosses could not pay. The suit was sent back. Clyde Ross did not go to the church program.[14]

There are of course multiple ways to read this paragraph. One is for meaning, as you learn about the Ross family's plight. Another is reading for structure, taking a view of how the sentences work together, creating and resolving dramatic tension. From this perspective, we want to point out one thing: as you read through the paragraph, you may notice something quite basic but also very important: the sentences vary in length. The shortest is only three words; the longest is nearly twenty. What effect does this variance cause? Longer sentences tend to build on themselves, complexifying the topic under discussion. This can be useful, as all those words work together to show relationships between words, ideas, moments, and to give a topic more color and detail. But they can also be confusing and exhausting to read. Shorter sentences, on the other hand, are easily digested and usually simpler to understand. But too many short sentences can feel repetitive, even jarring— like a rapid-fire machine gun. Thus, it's important to keep your sentence lengths varied and balanced. Now let's turn to a third way of reading. This third way is also structural, but it evaluates each sentence individually rather than considering their interrelations. It's detailed and exhaustive,

14. Ta-Nehisi Coates, "The Case for Reparations," *The Atlantic*, June 2014, https://www.theatlantic.com/magazine/archive/2014/06/the-case -for-reparations/361631/.

but doing this work will help you better understand your own writing, too.

Let's take that first sentence of the Coates text:

"The losses mounted."

Which kind of basic sentence is this? It's an independent clause with an intransitive verb. You might wonder more about how much or of what kind the losses are, or where they came from, which the rest of the paragraph will tell you, but on its own, "the losses mounted," is a complete thought.

If we turn to the second sentence, we see a bit more complexity:

"As sharecroppers, the Ross family saw their wages treated as the landlord's slush fund."

The first clause, before the comma, isn't a complete thought. It identifies a subject, but it doesn't tell us anything about what that subject does or how it relates. Because it's incomplete, we know it's a dependent clause and so can't be a sentence all on its own. Reading on, we see right away what that dependent clause is doing. "As sharecroppers" modifies what comes after it, "the Ross family." So the Ross family, which is the sentence's main subject, is modified by the prior dependent clause. They are sharecroppers.

We continue in this sentence, noticing a verb next: "saw." This verb ends up being the sentence's main action, but we don't yet know that. For now, all we have in this clause is a subject and a verb: "the Ross family saw." Is this clause independent? That depends on how we understand the verb "saw." Is it transitive or intransitive? Here you might recognize a truth about many verbs: they can play both transitive and intransitive roles. "The Ross family

saw" could be a complete thought, but in this case (and oftentimes), it's pointing beyond itself, to the next (or previous) phrase; here it's pointing to the next clause, what they
saw in their wages. The rest of the sentence functions as a
direct object for "saw," which is playing a transitive role,
pointing to what they saw. The rest of the sentence—"their
wages treated as the landlord's slush fund"—isn't quite a
complete thought, though it has noun phrases (wages,
landlord's slush fund) and a verb phrase ("treated"), so it's
a dependent clause.

If we wanted, we could continue on in just this way,
identifying each sentence's internal structure. For now,
though, let's note one other feature of Coates's writing and
then turn to another example text, one you may have seen
before.

For this last note, let's take up three of the shorter sentences: "The mailman arrived with the suit. The Rosses
could not pay. The suit was sent back." These simple sentences carry significant emotional weight; they're a list of
facts, but these facts matter because of what the suit
means to the Rosses. Coates emphasizes this meaning by
varying something called the sentence's "voice." There are
two general voices, active and passive.

Active Voice

In an active-voice sentence, the subject performs the verb's
action. The first sentence shows this kind of voice: *the mailman arrived*. Active-voice sentences are generally simpler
for readers to interpret. They often give writing "impact,"
because they tell the reader much of what they need to
understand what's happening. In this way, they tend to
keep a piece of writing moving along nicely. In contrast,
passive-voice sentences are those where the verb's action
happens to the sentence's subject. The sentence "the suit

was sent back" uses the passive voice. The suit isn't packing itself into a container and heading down to the post office. Instead, that's happening to it. Who's doing it? Well, that's left for the reader to figure out, infer, or imagine.

Generally speaking, you should use active-voice sentences. They're clearer and help the reader. But if this is so, why did a writer as good as Coates use passive voice for what happened to the suit? Because it indicates the Ross family's inability to act for themselves. The suit is sent back not because they don't want it but because they're unable to have it. Bad things are happening to them, and they're stuck. Coates's intentional use of the passive voice here makes the reader feel a little uneasy about freedom and agency, which end up being key topics for the rest of the text.

Now, let's look at one last text, also about freedom, which you've probably seen before:

> When in the Course of human events, it becomes necessary for one people to dissolve the political bands which have connected them with another, and to assume among the powers of the earth, the separate and equal station to which the Laws of Nature and of Nature's God entitle them, a decent respect to the opinions of mankind requires that they should declare the causes which impel them to the separation. . . . We hold these truths to be self-evident, that all men are created equal, that they are endowed by their Creator with certain unalienable Rights, that among these are Life, Liberty and the pursuit of Happiness.

This well-known passage is of course part of the introduction and preamble to the United States Declaration of Independence. You may have noticed that despite all those words and ideas, it's only two sentences. Because these words may be familiar to you—perhaps you've even memorized them—you likely have some idea of what they mean. But what if you didn't? What if this were your first time reading through? Would it be easy-going, or would you struggle? Our guess is that you'd struggle. We'd struggle, too: this text is written for majesty, not for ease of comprehension. Were Thomas Jefferson our student, we'd encourage him to use shorter sentences, though who knows what alternate history we'd have if our advice had been taken.

Dependent and Independent Clauses

Something else we can easily learn from Jefferson's preamble is how dependent clauses build upon one another. If we start reading from the top, we find a complete thought only at "it becomes necessary for one people to dissolve the political bands which have connected them with another." What comes before and after is all dependent clauses, explaining how the complete thought fits into Jefferson's theories of history, nature, and politics.

The second sentence starts right away with an independent clause: "We hold these truths to be self-evident." One wonders "which truths?" but that doesn't need to be cleared up for the sentence to be comprehensible. What follows is an exploration of truths, as a series of dependent clauses. It's possible to break up the rest of that sentence into many independent clauses: "All men are created equal. They are endowed by their Creator with certain unalienable Rights. Among these rights are Life, Liberty and the pursuit of Happiness." But that's not how Jefferson does it. Rather, he keeps the subsequent clauses dependent. What's the effect? As we read it, each subsequent clause builds in intensity as it explains and unpacks each of the prior ideas.

As we mentioned, this kind of structural reading, really digging into how each sentence works, is slow-going. We encourage you to keep practicing this skill, not only with class writings but also with other writers' words, including your own. Much as doctors need to understand how the body's various organs and functions interplay within a given system (digestive, circulatory, etc.), writers need to understand how sentences' pieces and parts fit together. As you begin to evaluate your own writing in this way, and in the other ways we're covering in this book, you might worry it won't ever match up to words and sentences like those Coates writes. That's understandable—but nothing to worry about. After all, Coates is one of the contemporary world's best nonfiction authors, and you're just starting out. Imagine how silly it'd feel to compare a Little Leaguer's swing of the bat against Babe Ruth's, or a kindergartener's artwork against the *Mona Lisa*. You wouldn't be too hard on that Little Leaguer or the child artist, so don't be too hard on yourself, either. Anne Lamott said, we think correctly, that "very few writers really know what they are doing until they have done it."[15] So do it. Try it. Remember to keep your sentences short and active. Look for those nouns and let them "do stuff" or "do their verbs."

EXERCISES

We want you to practice concision, so all four exercises below involve cutting, rephrasing, and combining your way into concision.

1. Did you find George Carlin's pleonastic paragraph funny? Good. Now suck all the humor out of Carlin's example by killing its pleonasms to death! In other words, remove all pleonasms. We hope that by playing

---

15. Lamott, *Bird by Bird: Some Instructions on Writing and Life*, 22.

Carlin's editor—an editor who dislikes humor—you're
able to exercise your skills at sniffing out redundancy,
repetition, echoing, duplication, and gratuitous reit-
eration.

2. Revise the following three sentences by folding prepositional phrases into adjectives. Examples:

> Sentence: Michelle is a famous *writer of memoirs*.
> Revision: Michelle is a famous *memoirist*.

> Sentence: She also writes poems *on historical topics*.
> Revision: She also writes *historical* poems.

   (i)   That pizzeria *next to the lake* burned down in June.
   (ii) The café *at the corner* burned down two weeks after
         the pizzeria burned down.
   (iii) When police found the arsonist, he was *under the
         influence of alcohol*.

3. Revise the following sentences for concision by using
a precise word for each italicized segment.
   (i)   Like owls, pessimistic philosophers are probably
         more *active at night* than *active during the day*.
   (ii) *Plato's famous Athenian teacher* was *put to death*.
   (iii) Critical thinking and *a phobia of confined spaces*
         express the same confidence that life is best out-
         side the box.

4. Combine into one sentence the following sentences
from Ernest Hemingway's introduction to *Men at War*:

"No. This book will not tell you how to die. This book
will tell you, though, how all men from the earliest
times we know have fought and died."[16]

---

16. Ernest Hemingway, ed., *Men at War: The Best War Stories of All Time*
(New York: Bramhall House, 1942), 5.

Chapter 8

THINKING THROUGH TO THE END

CLOSURE IN WRITING AND ARGUMENT

Endings have a certain power over us. The finale seems special, more meaningful—lasting. Many of us have a fascination with someone's dying words. Merely by being at the end, a word or sentence assumes a certain inexplicable weightiness. For this reason alone, readers can be positively upset by a bungled ending; a bungled ending can taint everything good that came before. In recent cultural memory, one may recall *Game of Thrones*. Eight seasons concluded in a clunker. *Game of Thrones* was botched. Game over. Other television series have suffered from similar clunky ends, including, in the estimation of some, the '90s classic *Seinfeld*.

Essays—either academic or popular—are bookended by an introduction and a conclusion. The conclusion can often be cut short by necessity: the due date is upon you and there is no time for elegant finishes. As John Steinbeck says in *East of Eden*, "In human affairs of danger and delicacy successful conclusion is sharply limited by hurry."[1] It is also possible that by the time you write the conclusion of a piece, you are sometimes so tired of the subject that your conclusion strikes you as an afterthought. But it shouldn't. Endings in a research paper may not play the same dramatic role they play in fiction, but they do hold a similar power. A weak conclusion can leave a bad

---

1. John Steinbeck, *East of Eden* (New York: Viking Press, 1952), 240.

taste, but more specifically, leave a reader feeling a certain lack of closure, as if the song has been cut off twenty seconds too soon, or the buzzer has sounded prematurely on the championship game. So do what every real champion does: finish strong.

A Satisfying Conclusion

Generally, two things are essential for the conclusion of a research paper. First, conclusions must in some way restate your thesis or summarize your findings. This does not mean giving a word-for-word restatement of your thesis copied-and-pasted into your conclusion, but a new, though not too divergent, phrasing of your thesis.

Consider the example:

> *Thesis*: I will argue that, for Friedrich Nietzsche, there are but two ways to affirm human existence, through the exercise of the will in activity, and through a radical acceptance (i.e., love) of life's conditions, of fate, even in complete frailty.

> *Conclusion*: At last, we watch the will to power fade—as all things do in life—only to see the love of fate take center stage for Nietzsche; these are the two guiding beacons in a fulfilling Nietzschean life.

The phrasing of the thesis and conclusion differ, but not significantly, and the conclusion is framed in such a way to remind a reader of the intellectual journey that they have made. Signal phrases in conclusions can give a reader a sense of closure: "in summary," "to sum up," "in conclusion," "ultimately," "therefore," "finally." While useful, these phrases, however, should be used sparingly since they are used by so many authors.

In addition to reframing the thesis, an effective conclusion highlights the practical significance and use of your thesis. How do you envision your thesis helping a reader? What counterarguments can now be decisively set aside? What further work might be done on the shoulders of your thesis? What deeper open questions has this exploration revealed? All of these questions might be ones that you gesture toward in developing your conclusion. Don't worry about answering the questions (that is for another paper and another time); the gesture should be enough to give your reader a lasting impression of your thesis's importance. And that is what you are aiming for in writing an effective conclusion: you want to make an imprint on a reader's mind in relation to your argument. First impressions are crucial, but last words are lasting.

We like to think about meaningful conclusions—in essays—as being similar to meaningful conclusions in life. At the end, astride the grave, you want, we think rather desperately, to say why all of your work has been worthwhile, to explain why living hasn't been more or less a waste of time. That is what you want to express in the end of your writing. As Virginia Woolf wrote in *The Waves*,

> "Now to sum it up," said Bernard. "Now to explain to you the meaning of my life. Since we do not know each other (though I met you once I think, on board a ship going to Africa), we can talk freely. The illusion is upon me that something adheres for a moment, has roundness, weight, depth, is completed. This, for the moment, seems to be my life. If it were possible, I would hand it you entire. I would break it off as one breaks off a bunch of grapes. I would say, 'Take it. This is my life.'"[2]

---

2. Virginia Woolf, *The Waves* (London: Hogarth Press, 1990), 158–59.

In writing a conclusion, you want to hand your "entire" argument to an audience, all at once, in a way that they can receive and carry on. You want to say to a reader: "Take it. It is yours now. It is worth carrying."

Closing Arguments

Let's get more concrete about endings. Academic essays must close with a sense of argumentative closure, a feeling achieved when a reader receives an argument that has been "buttoned up," meaning where the premises are once again, and for the last time, shown to support a particular thesis in a compelling way.

When a lawyer gives a closing argument, she is doing something very much akin to providing argumentative closure. Such closure is achieved when a speaker or writer reiterates, quickly, the premises of an argument and explains, in sum, why they lead to a particular conclusion or interpretation. In a closing argument, a lawyer argues the merits of a particular case, stating, "As we know from Witnesses A, B, and C's compelling testimony, Events X, Y, and Z occurred, which clearly establishes that Q and R should be held responsible in this case." In buttoning up your academic essays, you might want to take a lawyerly stance: laying out the factual evidence, restating the competency of your eyewitness (scholars in the field or research methods used), and explaining the way that the facts and testimony lend credence to exactly one conclusion: yours.

CRAFTING THE ENDING

Endings are determined by what precedes them. The expression "never look back" is terrible advice for wrapping up an argumentative essay. The style, form, voice, stance,

Get to Work

EVALUATING AND DRAFTING CONCLUSIONS

1. Pick one scholarly and one popular essay. Read each through and carefully evaluate the conclusion. Explain the extent to which the conclusions summarize the thesis of the essay, emphasize the practical import, give the "entire" argument, or craft lawyer-like closing arguments. It may be the case that the conclusions from the writer of the essay you select do a poor job. If that is the case, take the opportunity to explain their deficiency.

2. Select one scholarly essay. Print it out. Before reading it, remove the last two paragraphs without reading them. Read the essay and write the last two paragraphs of the piece. After you are finished writing, compare and contrast the two sets of paragraphs, using the standards of a "satisfying conclusion."

and purpose of a conclusion will depend on what you have written in your body paragraphs. You want to make sure that it is tied closely to the overall theme and objective of your essay. This is also to suggest that there is no single "right way" to write an ending. There are, however, a number of tricks of the trade that we have developed over the years that have assisted us at times when an essay seems without end.

Tips for Writing Conclusions

1. *Reread your essay.* Take special note of the following features that you might want to elaborate on in the final moments of your essay and argument. An elaboration often just amounts to showing the reader some deeper

meaning of a message you have already conveyed, so keep an eye out for the following in your rereading:

a. A figure or character in a story who performs an action or makes a speech that has not been discussed in your essay, but exemplifies perfectly the points that you are making.

b. A quotation that deserves to be restated for emphasis and revisited as a way of buttoning up an argument.

c. A particular pivotal premise or piece of evidence that you believe "seals" the argument nicely and succinctly.

d. An aspect of the problem or analytic question that went unresolved in the course of your essay.

2. *Leave the reader with a story or personal example of how your argument might play out in real life*, making sure that the story demonstrates various aspects of your argument.

3. *Leave your reader with a quotation from another source* that reveals the scope, depth, or historical significance of the issue or argument you are taking up.

4. *Leave your reader with short, memorable sentences.*

5. *Leave your reader with a series of questions* that might lead to future thought or research.

6. *Leave your reader with a sense of the personal significance of the argument*; the conclusion is one of the places where personal, first-person narrative is used to great effect. Similarly, a conclusion might be a time to "go meta," in other words, to take a perspective above and beyond your argument, looking down and commenting on what you have tried to accomplish or what drew you to the topic in the first place.

Some instructors teach that a conclusion should take a pyramidal form, with a very narrow, specific claim set out first (occasionally the restatement of the thesis), which leads to broader and more general "takeaways" as the conclusion proceeds. This might work for you, but make sure that both your specific points and general "takeaways" make an impact on your reader in a way that your body paragraphs do not. Your conclusion must be more forceful and memorable than the rest for the essay, save perhaps the introductory hook. So, if you finish an essay and you are bored in rereading it to the end, change your conclusion and revisit the body paragraphs.

Concluding Catastrophes

At several points in *Thinking through Writing*, we have adopted what medieval scholars called the *via negativa*, the "negative way." When talking about what a thesis should be, we started with what a thesis was not. And when describing great conclusions, it is helpful to address the construction of very bad ones. So here are some concluding catastrophes. Avoid them at all costs.

1. *Avoid opening a conclusion with the signal phrases "in conclusion," "in sum," or "at the end of our discussion."* These three come across as especially trite. You may want to embed a signal phrase in the conclusion, but make sure that it is not condescending to a reader's ear.
2. *Avoid simple summary.* Your conclusion should gesture only to the high points and broader significance of your thesis, not to every contour of your argument.
3. *Avoid introducing new information.* You can introduce a new quote or a new final example of your point, but the conceptual work in a paper needs to be done in the body paragraphs, not in the conclusion. Make sure that you do not mention counterarguments at the end of your essay: it is, after all, your essay, and not your interlocutor's.
4. *Avoid qualifying your thesis.* There is a temptation for authors to reach the end of an essay and think "God,

this is total crap." They then say so to their readers: "I claim no expertise over this topic, but I have tried my best to argue. . . ." Don't undercut your argument with false humility. You have written something you believe in and defended it to your best abilities. Trust thyself.

5. *Avoid droning on.* Conclusions must be proportional to the length of the essay: approximately one-tenth to one-eighth of the essay's total length.

FINAL TIPS ON WRITING

Before we bid you goodbye and set you off on your life as a writer, we want to leave you with a few parting words. First, let us be clear: you can return to this book whenever you like, whenever you write. Second, you will, whether you like it or not, have a life as a reader and writer. Your social and professional life will depend on your ability to communicate—often in writing—and this short handbook will, we hope, see you through the moments in which you might be at a loss for words. There are technical tricks that you can master that will help: shortcuts in writing introductions and transitions, guidelines for making arguments and using sources, rules of the road in using grammar and closing with an impact. But there are also gentle suggestions that most writing handbooks fail to make regarding how to live and how to think creatively. You might get these tips in an advanced writing workshop—which we have led many times—or if you hired a writing coach. But in the event that you never have a coach or attend a workshop, here goes.

The Write Place

Our friend Andre Dubus III, the best-selling author of *The House of Sand and Fog*, recently told us, "You've got to find your own place to write." Several years ago, he built a house on the shores of a New England river and, at its center, a soundproof room—six feet by eight feet—that he calls "the cave." Dubus retreats to the cave religiously, almost every morning for three hours. After listening to Dubus, John decided to make a cave of his own, by emptying an upstairs closet and dragging a desk inside. He goes there every time he needs to get away from the two oversized dogs that make writing at home occasionally impossible. Here is the point: sometimes it is hard to hear yourself think, and therefore hard to write, so sometimes you need some very precious silence and the comfort of an environment that you call your own. We recommend Virginia Woolf's *A Room of One's Own*, maybe the most succinct defense of a writer's sacred privacy, especially for women, who were rarely allowed even the freedom of their own room, and still today must push back against infringements. You need to hear the words in your head before you write them out. So, ask yourself:

1. Do I need silence to write?
2. Do I need a window to write?
3. What do I like to look at when I write?
4. Do I like to sit at a particular chair or in a particular coffeehouse?
5. Do I write best when alone or when surrounded by other writers and researchers?
6. Do I need a particular tool—like a favorite pen or notebook to write?

Some writers need a little noise—soft chatter, the whir of espresso machines, and the clink of teacups on saucers.[3] French existentialist writers, such as Simone de Beauvoir and Jean-Paul Sartre, wrote copiously in the bustling cafés of Paris. Some writers need neither silence nor the soft

---

3. There is even a website for lovers of café noise, coffitivity.com, which "recreates the ambient sounds of a café to boost your creativity and help you work better." You can also find countless café "ambience" videos on YouTube!

ambience of public spaces; they can write almost anywhere. Ray Bradbury suggested that the locale, or even the
presence or absence of distractions, didn't matter to him.
Just having a typewriter, any typewriter, was enough.

> I can work anywhere. I wrote in bedrooms and liv-
> ing rooms when I was growing up with my parents
> and my brother in a small house in Los Angeles.
> I worked on my typewriter in the living room, with
> the radio and my mother and dad and brother all
> talking at the same time. Later on, when I wanted to
> write *Fahrenheit 451*, I went up to UCLA and found a
> basement typing room where, if you inserted ten
> cents into the typewriter, you could buy thirty min-
> utes of typing time.[4]

On the other hand, Joan Didion, when she was knee-deep
in a book, commented that she actually needed to sleep in
the same room with the manuscript, to wake up and work
on it immediately.[5] You may find a spot that works particularly well for a time—maybe a particular corner of a
restaurant—but then you get stuck in a paragraph or transition. Physically take yourself somewhere else. It may
even be a good idea to try to write in a very unusual place
to jolt yourself out of writer's anxiety.

The Write Time

The time of day to write is as important as finding a particular writer's nook. Many writers we know are early

---

4. Ray Bradbury, "The Art of Fiction No. 203," interview by Sam Weller,
Paris Review, no. 192 (Spring 2010): https://www.theparisreview.org
/interviews/6012/the-art-of-fiction-no-203-ray-bradbury.

5. Joan Didion, "The Art of Fiction No. 71," interview by Linda Kuehl,
Paris Review, no. 74 (Fall–Winter 1978): https://www.theparisreview
.org/interviews/3439/the-art-of-fiction-no-71-joan-didion.

risers and do their best work before breakfast—just coffee and a single light in the living room will do. Others are
night owls: Jack Kerouac famously would start at mid-
night and work through till dawn, fueled by alcohol, which
we do not recommend. Give yourself some space, both
physically and chronologically. Some of the best writers
swear by a religious daily routine, the word "daily" being
key; they keep themselves mentally and creatively lim-
ber by consistent "writing workouts." Other writers are
comfortable with writing only when the spirit moves
then, but we think that this approach is not particularly
helpful for beginning writers who might be avoiding a task
at hand. So, keep a schedule and adjust the schedule if you
find it to be stifling rather than inspiring or productive.

Read, Write, Type, Revise, Repeat

Some authors prime themselves with a little inspirational
reading, and then find it helpful to write drafts in different
mediums—on a white board, on paper, on the computer, in
specific notebooks. Dubus, for example, starts his day by
reading a bit of poetry. It doesn't matter if he is writing a
gritty novel about ex-convicts—he starts with poetry. Next,
he types out everything he has written from the previous
day; he writes his first draft longhand on paper. This allows
him to refresh his memory of the recent moves he made
and to revise the work as he now sees fit. After the typing
is finished, he goes back to his pencil and notebook to craft
the next few pages.

Talk to Yourself

The instruction to talk to yourself might seem crazy. OK,
it is a little bizarre. But find a safe space—the bathroom
stall, an empty car, a gentle jog in the woods—and have at
it. Speech is roughly grammatically correct, so just start

with a few sentences about your topic. When you listen to yourself, you are often able to catch awkward phrasing, passive (weak) voice, and gaps in your reasoning. You will also hear places where you need to provide additional support. If you are doing a close reading of a text and uncover a particular passage of interest, take the time to explain its significance *out loud* to yourself. Reciting aloud has the added advantage of anchoring words in your memory, so when you get back to your keyboard, all you will have to do is transcribe what is already in your head.

Make a List

Very long pieces of writing consist of a whole bunch of teeny-tiny pieces of writing. Break things up into subsections of similar length. Make a list of these subsections (we like spreadsheets for this purpose). Reserve a column for word count, another to mark whether the section is drafted, and another to mark it as finished. By making writing segmental, you create manageable chunks of work, which can be dispatched relatively quickly. By finishing sections, one after another, you can propel yourself into progress and the sense that you are close to finishing the work on the whole. Making this sort of list also makes it easier to write nonlinearly, meaning to write sections that strike your fancy in no particular order. Maybe you are in the mood to discuss a counterargument in section 7 today; tomorrow section 2 on historical context. You get to pick.

Make a Log

Take account of your progress as a writer day to day. How many words did you produce, of what quality, for what purpose? Where were you and at what time? What did you eat and how did you sleep the night before? And what do you feel? Did you have any particularly good conversations about your writing? Did you do anything very enjoyable or very depressing on the day of your writing? Answers to these questions might not seem to bear directly on the art of writing, but if you keep a log over a long enough period of time, certain patterns will emerge. Maybe you write very well on a day when you eat a chocolate scone, or more realistically, when you have dinner with a loved one at the end of the writing session. Maybe you work very well on an empty stomach or when you get eight hours of sleep. Or perhaps you work very well on no sleep at all (although if that is the case, we suggest, from experience, that you need to be wary of this trend). In any event, you won't be able to monitor these patterns unless you document them. So, keep a writing log.

Go for a Walk

Don't take your cell phone with you. Don't put your watch on. Just walk for a while. Or run if you like. The expression "thinking on your feet" is literal and meaningful: a large number of the best writers and thinkers have been great walkers. Sometimes you need to get away from your usual surroundings in order to think freely or question the assumptions of daily life, two prerequisites of exceptional writing. Don't take our word for it. Just go for a stroll. You may walk your way out of writer's block or arrive at a conclusion that has eluded you for many days in your writer's nook.

Creative Procrastination

This is just what it sounds like. It is procrastination that actually creates something. First, you need two separate writing projects. Three or four will also work, but be honest and modest about your workload. Start one essay, and when you get bored or stuck, turn to the other. Make sure they are significantly different so it doesn't feel like you are going in circles. You also have to make sure that both writing projects are viable: they are the sort that can be submitted and published or graded. Part of the beauty of avoiding some work by doing other work is that you are still doing work. But you feel, in this case, a sense of control you might not in other contexts.

Make Like Joyce

So, you are in the throes writing a very ugly essay: nothing, and we mean *nothing*, is good about this essay. You have worked on it for several weeks and it is not salvageable. Print out two copies of the essay. Delete the file. Go ahead. Make sure you keep all of your source material and background research. Send one of the copies to a distant friend. Burn the other one.

James Joyce was so despondent after receiving more than twenty rejections of his book *Stephen Hero* that he burned the sucker. His family suffered pretty serious burns trying to save it from the fire. What they managed to save became one of the most famous books of the twentieth century: *A Portrait of the Artist as a Young Man*. Burning something, anything really, has a liberatory feel to it. Nothing is left behind save for the memory of what was lost. And that might allow you to start again freshly on a piece of writing without the same old hang-ups and false-steps. Then again, by sending a copy to a friend, you always have the option of using the material again if you see fit.

Ignore Distractions

Usually, the expression is "avoid distractions," but great writers are often masters of ignoring them. That is to say that the world around them can be going to hell in a hand-basket, and there they sit at their computer or writing desk for hours that could be spent in a million other different ways. This makes writers sound like irresponsible jerks, and sometimes we are, but life often has a way of forgiving the laser focus of a writer if he or she is clear-headed enough to return to the world when the muse departs. Obviously, don't push it. But also, don't allow everything to come in the way of you and your writing. You need a little privacy, what the Victorians called "reserve," a creative room of your own.

Follow the Scent

Let's end with a tip from Andre Dubus III. Many writing instructors will suggest that you employ an outline, and that is not bad advice, but recently he commented,

> I love that line from E. L. Doctorow: "Writing a novel is like driving at night. You can only see as far as your headlights," but you keep going until you get there. I've learned over the years to just report back anything that I see in front of the headlights: Are they yellow stripes or white? What's on the side of the road? Is there vegetation? What kind? What's the weather? What are the sounds? If I capture the experience all along the way, the structure starts to reveal itself. My guiding force and principle for shaping the story is to just follow the headlights. That's how the architecture is revealed.[6]

Dubus's point also suggests something essential about thinking, research, and writing on the whole (not just in writing a novel). You may have some plan about how things

---

6. Andre Dubus III, "Do Not Think, Dream," in *Light the Dark: Writers on Creativity, Inspiration, and the Artistic Process*, ed. Joe Fassler (New York: Penguin Books, 2017), 63.

are going to go in the course of crafting an essay, and that is all fine and good, but many times, you actually have no idea where the research will lead you until you sift through it with the utmost care. Keep your headlights on, or follow the scent of the interesting questions, perplexing premises, and tantalizing conclusions, and see where they lead. Remember that writing—like life—is a recursive process of revision and reevaluation rather than a point A to point B trek.

FINAL THOUGHTS: THE PERFECT ESSAY IN THE END

The Perfect Essay

We don't want you, much less expect you, to become a flawless writer or thinker. All the tips in the world won't guarantee perfection. Humans make mistakes, and that is invariably for the best, for what would life be if everything were sorted out entirely? Instead, we want you to become *better*: to think more clearly and deeply, to express your ideas concisely and powerfully, to be understood and heeded, to become the sort of thoughtful person you often wish to be. Becoming better presumes error, but also the consistent, let us say courageous, willingness to overcome it. If this seems daunting, let us provide a final perspective on the task of becoming a better writer, thinker, and person.

Looking back on too many years of education, John can identify one truly impossible teacher. She cared about him, and his intellectual life, even when he didn't. Her expectations were high—impossibly so. She was an English teacher. She was also his mother.

When good students turn in an essay, they dream of their instructor returning it to them in exactly the same condition, save for a single word added in the margin of the final page: "flawless." This dream came true for John one afternoon in the ninth grade. Of course, John had heard that genius could show itself at an early age, so he was only slightly taken aback that he had achieved perfection as a fourteen-year-old. Obviously, he did what any professional writer would do: John hurried off to spread the good news. He didn't get very far. The first person he told was his mother.

John's mother, Becky, who is just shy of five feet tall, is normally incredibly soft-spoken, but on the rare occasion when she gets angry, she is terrifying. He's not sure if she was more upset by his hubris or by the fact that his English teacher had let his ego become so inflated. In any event, John's mom and her red pen showed him how deeply flawed a "flawless" essay could be. At the time, he's sure she thought she was teaching him about mechanics, transitions, structure, style, and voice. But what he learned—and what he would like to pass on to you—was a deeper lesson about the nature of creative criticism and the ultimate goal of writing and thinking.

First off, it hurts. Genuine criticism, the type that leaves an indelible mark on you as a writer, also leaves an existential imprint on you as a person. Some people say that a writer should never take criticism personally. That's rubbish. Criticism, at its best, is deeply personal, and it gets to the heart of why we write the way we do. Perhaps you're a narcissist who secretly resents your audience. Or an elitist who expects Herculean feats of your reader. Or a know-it-all who can't admit that stylistic repetition is sometimes annoying. Or a wallflower who hides behind sparklingly meaningless modifiers. Or an affirmation junkie who's the first to brag about a flawless essay.

Unfortunately, as John's mother explained, you can be all of these things at once. Her red pen had made something painfully clear: to become a better writer, he first had to become a better person. Well before John ever read it, his mother expressed the meaning of Walt Whitman's "Song of Myself." And he faced the disturbing suggestion that his song was no good.

The intimate nature of genuine criticism implies something about the person who is able to give it, namely, someone who knows you well enough to show you how your psychic life is getting in the way of good writing. Conveniently, they're also the people who care enough to see you through the traumatic aftermath of this realization. For John, the aftermath took the form of his first and worst encounter with writer's block.

It lasted three years.

John's mother's criticism had shown him that when you make the introspective descent into yourself that writing requires, you're not always pleased by what you find. But John was lucky enough to find a critic and teacher who was willing to make the journey of writing with him. According to Plutarch, "to offer objections against a discourse which has been delivered is not difficult, but very easy; but to set up a better against it is a very laborious task."[7] John is sure he wrote essays in the later years of high school without his mother's guidance, but he can't recall them. What he remembers, however, is how she took up the "very laborious" work of ongoing criticism.

There are two ways to interpret Plutarch when he suggests that a critic should be able to "set up a better" discourse. In a straightforward sense, he could mean that critics must be more talented than the artists they critique. John's mother was well covered on this count. (She denies it, but she's still a much, much better writer than he is.)

---

7. Plutarch, *Moralia*, vol. 1, trans. Frank Cole Babbitt, Loeb Classical Library 197 (Cambridge, MA: Harvard University Press, 1927), 221.

But perhaps Plutarch is suggesting something slightly different. Genuine criticism creates a precious opening for authors to become better on their own terms—a process that's often excruciating, but also almost always meaningful.

John's mom said that she would help him with his writing, but that first he had to help himself. For each assignment, he was to write the best essay he could. Real criticism isn't meant to find obvious mistakes, so if she found any—the type he could have found on his own—he had to start from scratch. From scratch. Once the essay was "flawless," she would take an evening to walk him through his errors. That was when true criticism, the type that changed him as a person, began.

She chided him as a pseudo-sophisticate when he included obscure references and professional jargon. She had no patience for clever but useless extended metaphors. "Writers can't bluff their way through ignorance." That was news to him—he'd need to find another way to structure his daily existence. She trimmed back his flowery language, drew lines through his exclamation marks, and argued for the value of understatement. "John," she almost whispered. He leaned in to hear her: "I can't hear you when you shout at me." So, he stopped shouting and bluffing, and slowly his writing improved.

Somewhere along the way John set aside his hopes of writing that flawless essay. But perhaps he missed something important in his mother's lessons about creativity and perfection. Perhaps the point of writing the flawless essay was not to give up, but to never willingly finish. Whitman repeatedly reworked "Song of Myself" between 1855 and 1891. Repeatedly. We do our absolute best with a piece of writing, and come as close as we can to the ideal. And, for the time being, we settle. In critique, however, we are forced to depart, to give up the perfection we thought we had achieved for the chance of being even a little bit better. This is the lesson John took from his mother that he passes on to you at the end of *Thinking through Writing*: if perfection were possible, it wouldn't be motivating.

In the End

In the end, no essay is perfect, yet some are deeply and enduringly satisfying. Readers return to their favorite essays, again and again, at least in part, to scour the inconsistencies that emerge, the puzzles and mysteries that abide, the questions that have been revealed in a subtle examination of a topic. This is not to say that an author tries to leave loose ends, but rather that topics worth investigating are rarely the sort that can be fully explored in a single essay or by a single author. An essay, in the sense given by its French origin, *essai*, is simply an attempt at something, and the most valiant attempts strive after something out of reach, like achieving clarity and insight about the obscurest questions.

Writing is always an attempt in another important respect, one that we hope has not been lost on you in the course of *Thinking through Writing*. It is the attempt to overcome a loneliness built into the very structure of human and intellectual life. Human existence often feels like a solitary affair. Crowds swarm the plaza, classmates stir in the surrounding seats, children call from the other room; a friend brings you coffee as you work—but you are, for better and for worse, alone. At least it often seems that way. The choices that you make in life are the choices *you*, and you alone, make in life. Your thoughts arise slowly from a place deep inside you, or appear suddenly at the back of your head. But in any event, the thoughts are yours and not ever your neighbor's. You will die and your thoughts will come to an end.

Unless you write them down.

Writing is always directed toward a meeting of the minds, to bridge the seeming gulf between our "tiny skull-sized kingdoms" as David Foster Wallace would have it.[8] And it is directed to a future, both immediate and distant, which is not our own. Those who read your words—who think them through, across the page—can carry them on. Writing is thinking made visible, such that it can be thought through, endlessly, by someone else. And this is nothing short of a miracle. Now you know the stakes of thinking through writing: writing clearly, forcefully, honestly, and authentically is a matter of preserving and passing on what is most essential to each of us, the questions and answers that mold a human life.

EXERCISES

1. Guided by the "Avoid X" suggestions we made in "Concluding Catastrophes" (see pages 239–40), improve the following concluding paragraph:

   In conclusion, Nietzsche affirmed life. Well, at least that's what I tried to show, perhaps poorly. Nietzsche not only affirmed life, but held that there are two ways to do so, through the exercise of the will in activity, and through a radical acceptance of life's conditions. There is a counterargument, which I didn't address in the essay, which holds that there are three ways to affirm life in Nietzschean thought. But if you consider the second sentence of the tenth paragraph, where I stated that "Nietzsche opposes

---

8. David Foster Wallace, *This Is Water: Some Thoughts, Delivered on a Significant Occasion about Living a Compassionate Life* (New York: Little, Brown, 2009), 117.

simple dichotomies," then maybe I was making that same "counterargument" myself. Well, let's move on from that and still assume two ways of affirmation. At last, we watch the will to power fade—as all things do in life—only to see the love of fate take center stage for Nietzsche; these are the two guiding beacons in a fulfilling Nietzschean life. It seems.

2. Put us to the test. In two paragraphs, assess our concluding paragraph, the one that begins "Writing is always directed toward a meeting of the minds [. . .]." Did we follow our own advice? Did we contradict our advice in any way? Interrogate our paragraph. What did you like or not like about it, or better, what do you think was strong and effective or not? You are now in the driver's seat; you have always been in the driver's seat, but now, after all our "driving" lessons, it is safe to tell you that the keys have always been in your pocket! So have at us! Evaluate our work.

3. For those feeling especially adventurous, rewrite our concluding paragraph. Make it your own. The both of us wish deeply that your own voice come out now, because you are a unique being, a person who has never existed before and will not come again, whose intricate history and special future will never be duplicated, and thus whose voice and point of view is absolutely rare, if only it would come out and speak, come out and think out loud through writing.

ACKNOWLEDGMENTS

John would like to thank a host of amazing instructors, editors, and fellow writers who have, over the years, helped him think through his own writing (in no particular order): Patricia Meyer Spacks, Peter Aldinger, Derren Brown, Eileen Pollack, Clancy Martin, Megan Marshall, Chloe Cooper-Jones, Ileene Smith, Rob Tempio, Adam Kirsch, Gary Rosen, Peter Catapano, Bruce Falconer, Alex Kafka, Andrea Wulf, Cris Moore, Mrs. Ritter, Dave Emes, Douglas Anderson, John Traphagan, John Banville, and his mother, Becky Griffith Kaag. He is deeply indebted to the many interviewees and reviewers who graciously contributed their time to *Thinking through Writing*, and to the unflagging guidance provided by Matt Rohal at Princeton University Press. As always, he could not have written without the support of his wife, Kathleen, and their two kids, Becca and Henry. Finally, he would like to thank the small army of students with whom he has had the honor to work—side by side, essay after essay—over sixteen years of teaching.

Jonathan wishes to thank his mother, Dr. Robin Poe, for being the best English teacher he could have asked for in his younger years. To his father, Steven van Belle, Jonathan owes his sense of a balanced and cheerful rationality. Jonathan also wishes to thank another Steven, Steven A. Miller, for his comradeship in the trenches of English curriculum development. To his brother, Christopher, for the inestimable value of his role as a diabolical Socrates. He owes yet more to the creators of Microsoft Word, Google Docs, Purdue Online Writing Lab, and his 2015 iMac with macOS Monterey. To all such toolmakers, he sends his praise. He would like to acknowledge also his miniature schnauzer, Nietzsche, for the hourly reports; a good bark clears the mind—which is ideal for writing. To Matt Rohal, he offers a long hug and the deepest appreciation. Finally, Jonathan sends his love to his wife Zuriel, for whom this Belle tolls.

BIBLIOGRAPHY

American Psychological Association. "About APA." Last updated January 2022. https://www.apa.org/about.

Aristotle. *Introductory Readings*. Translated with introduction, notes, and glossary by Terence Irwin and Gail Fine. Indianapolis: Hackett, 1996.

Atwood, Margaret. *The Blind Assassin*. New York: Anchor Books, 2001.

Baker, Nicholson. *U and I: A True Story*. New York: Random House, 1991.

Barzun, Jacques. *From Dawn to Decadence: 500 Years of Western Cultural Life*. New York: HarperCollins, 2000.

Bierce, Ambrose. *The Unabridged Devil's Dictionary*. Athens: University of Georgia Press, 2002.

Bradbury, Ray. "The Art of Fiction No. 203." By Sam Weller. *Paris Review*, no. 192 (Spring 2010): https://www.theparisreview.org/interviews/6012/the-art-of-fiction-no-203-ray-bradbury.

Bukowski, Charles. *The Last Night of the Earth Poems*. New York: Ecco, 2002.

Butler, Smedley D. *War Is a Racket*. Port Townsend, WA: Feral House, 2003.

Carlin, George. *When Will Jesus Bring the Pork Chops?* New York: Hyperion, 2004.

Clark, Walter Houston. *Chemical Ecstasy: Psychedelic Drugs and Religion*. New York: Sheed and Ward, 1969.

Coates, Ta-Nehisi. "The Case for Reparations." *The Atlantic*, June 2014. https://www.theatlantic.com/magazine/archive/2014/06/the-case-for-reparations/361631/.

Didion, Joan. "The Art of Fiction No. 71." By Linda Kuehl. *Paris Review*, no. 74 (Fall–Winter 1978): https://www.theparisreview.org/interviews/3439/the-art-of-fiction-no-71-joan-didion.

Dubus, Andre, III. "Do Not Think, Dream." In *Light the Dark: Writers on Creativity, Inspiration, and the Artistic Process*, edited by Joe Fassler, 61–68. New York: Penguin Books, 2017.

Dyer, Geoff. *Out of Sheer Rage: Wrestling with D. H. Lawrence*. New York: North Point Press, 1997.

Emerson, Ralph Waldo. *Self-Reliance and Other Essays*. Mineola, NY: Dover, 1993.

Epicurus. *Letter to Pythocles*. In *The Art of Happiness*, translated by George K. Strodach. New York: Penguin Books, 2012.

Gorman, Amanda. *The Hill We Climb: An Inaugural Poem for the Country*. New York: Viking,2021.

Hemingway, Ernest, ed. *Men at War: The Best War Stories of All Time*. New York: Bramhall House, 1942.

Hesiod. *"Works and Days" and "Theogony."* Translated by Stanley Lombardo. Indianapolis: Hackett, 1993.

Hurston, Zora Neale. *Dust Tracks on a Road*. New York: HarperPerennial, 1996.

Jonson, Ben. *Timber, or Discoveries Made Upon Men and Matter*. Edited with introduction and notes by Felix E. Schelling. Boston: Ginn & Company, 1892.

Kaag, John. *Hiking with Nietzsche: On Becoming Who You Are*. New York: Farrar, Stauss and Giroux, 2018.

King, Martin Luther, Jr. "Letter from Birmingham Jail." In *Why We Can't Wait*, 76–95. New York: Signet Books, 1964.

King, Stephen. "A Preface in Two Parts." In *The Stand*, ix–xii. New York: Anchor Books, 2012.

Lamott, Anne. *Bird by Bird: Some Instructions on Writing and Life*. New York: Anchor Books, 1995.

Macklem, Gayle L. *Boredom in the Classroom: Addressing Student Motivation, Self-Regulation, and Engagement in Learning*. New York: Springer International, 2015.

Malcolm, Janet. *The Silent Woman: Sylvia Plath & Ted Hughes*. New York: Knopf, 1994.

Marshall, Megan. *Elizabeth Bishop: A Miracle for Breakfast*. Boston: Houghton Mifflin Harcourt, 2017.

Meriwether, James B., and Michael Millgate, eds. *Lion in the Garden: Interviews with William Faulkner, 1926–1962*. Lincoln: University of Nebraska Press, 1980.

National Archives and Records Administration. "Thomas Jefferson to John Adams, 17 May 1818." Accessed January 4, 2024. https://founders.archives.gov/documents/Jefferson/03-13-02-0042.

Nietzsche, Friedrich. *The Complete Works of Friedrich Nietzsche*. Vol. 9, *Ecce Homo*. Stanford: Stanford University Press, 2021.

Nietzsche, Friedrich. *The Complete Works of Friedrich Nietzsche*. Vol. 9, *Nietzsche Contra Wagner*. Stanford: Stanford University Press, 2021.

Nietzsche, Friedrich. *Thus Spake Zarathustra*. Translated by Thomas Common. New York: Heritage Press, 1967.

Plato. *Phaedrus*. Translated by Walter Hamilton. New York: Penguin Books, 1995.

Plutarch. *Moralia*. Vol. 1. Translated by Frank Cole Babbitt. Loeb Classical Library 197. Cambridge, MA: Harvard University Press, 1927.

Price, Lucien, comp. *Dialogues of Alfred North Whitehead*. Boston: Little, Brown, 1954.

Rumi. *The Essential Rumi*. Translated by Coleman Barks. New York: HarperCollins, 1995.

Ruskin, John. *A Joy For Ever*. 2nd ed. London: George Allen, 1895.

Schopenhauer, Arthur. *Arthur Schopenhauer: Philosophical Writings*. Translated by Virginia Cutrufelli. New York: Continuum, 1994.

Singer, Peter. "Famine, Affluence, and Morality." *Philosophy and Public Affairs* 1, no. 3 (Spring 1972): 229–43.

Sojourner Truth (Isabella Baumfree). Ohio Women's Rights Convention speech as transcribed by Marius Robinson, *Anti-slavery Bugle*, June 21, 1851. Sourced in *Chronicling America: Historic American Newspapers*, Library of Congress. https://chroniclingamerica.loc.gov/lccn/sn830 35487/1851-06-21/ed-1/seq-4/.

Stafford, William. *Writing the Australian Crawl: Views on the Writer's Vocation*. Ann Arbor: University of Michigan Press, 1978.

Steinbeck, John. *East of Eden*. New York: Viking Press, 1952.

Sunstein, Cass R. *On Rumor: How Falsehoods Spread, Why We Believe Them, and What Can Be Done*. Princeton, NJ: Princeton University Press, 2014.

Taylor, George R., ed. *Integrating Quantitative and Qualitative Methods in Research*. 2nd ed. Lanham, MD: University Press of America, 2005.

Wallace, David Foster. *This Is Water: Some Thoughts, Delivered on a Significant Occasion about Living a Compassionate Life*. New York: Little, Brown, 2009.

Whitehead, Alfred North. *The Aims of Education and Other Essays*. Rev. ed. London: Williams & Norgate, 1950.

Winokur, Jon, comp. *Advice to Writers*. New York: Pantheon, 1999.

Woolf, Virginia. *The Waves*. London: Hogarth Press, 1990.

Wu, Katherine J. "Grizzly Bears Are Mostly Vegan." *The Atlantic*. January 10, 2024. https://www.theatlantic.com /science/archive/2024/01/grizzly-bear-california -carnivore-meat-eating/677070/.

Xenophon. *Memorabilia*. Translated by E. C. Marchant. Loeb Classical Library 168. Cambridge, MA: Harvard University Press, 2013.

INDEX

active voice, 217–18, 228–29

Adams, John, 156

ad hominem fallacy, 69, 75–76

adjectives: defined, 223; linking verbs and, 223–24; replacing prepositional phrases with, 214, 232

Affirming a Disjunct, 70

AI-generated writing, 195

Ain't I a Woman (Truth), 20–22, 115

Albee, Edward, 24–25

Alessandri, Mariana, 51–52

alphanumeric outline, 98–100

analogy, arguments from, 58–61

analysis, 36–38

analytic questions: basic features of, 38; crafting of, 38–39; exercise about, 49–50; honing of, 40–41; as motivating for the reader, 39, 107, 134; in peer review, 134; for potential mentor, 132; six cardinal virtues of, 38–39; thesis as answer to, 42, 44, 47–48, 107; unresolved, 238; about yourself, 151. *See also* questions

annotations, 28, 32–33

anxiety, 156–57; managing, 161–64, 242. *See also* writer's block

APA style, 182–83, 186–89

argument from design, 59–61

arguments: from analogy, 58–61; Aristotle's three types of persuasion in, 4–5; cause and, 61–66; defined, 51;

exercises about, 82–85; motivation of, 77–82; soundness and, 57–58, 82–84; validity and, 55–57, 69, 82–84. *See also* conclusion of argument; premises

argumentum ad hominem, 69, 75–76

argumentum ad hominem tu quoque, 76–77

Aristophanes, 128

Aristotle, 4–5, 78

arrogant writing, 137, 154

Atwood, Margaret, 127

audience, 121–27; close reading and, 31; coauthor's perspective on, 130; exercises about, 126, 139; as free to turn elsewhere, 122; hooking, 104–7, 118–19; known or unknown, 122–23; motivating, 39, 77–82, 107, 134; of multiple different parts, 123; questions to ask yourself about, 124–25; of rhetorical situation, 19, 20; size of, 121; three ways to persuade, 4–5; topic sentence commanding attention of, 115; value of essay for, 125–27

authenticity, 155–56

author-date system, 189

background information: avoided in the hook, 106. *See also* context

Baker, Nicholson, 142

Barzun, Jacques, 178–79, 181